bob flowerdew

the no-work garden

bob flowerdew

the no-work garden

getting the most out of
your garden for the
least amount of work

This book is dedicated to all those who love gardening but have never been able to find enough time

The daisy chain

Taking an albatross for a garland of flowers I hung it round my neck
imagining its scent and form could my life and soul bedeck.
Instead it robbed me of my hours and drove me mad with flies
but rather than admit mistake; I still listen to its lies...

from *The pulpit and the potting shed: poems of the brothers Flowerdew*, 2000

This paperback edition published in 2005 by SILVERDALE BOOKS
An imprint of Bookmart Ltd, Registered number 2372865
Trading as Bookmart Limited, Blaby Road, Wigston, Leicester, LE18 4SE

First published in Great Britain in 2002 by Kyle Cathie Limited

ISBN 1 84509 132 9

Text © 2002 Bob Flowerdew
Special photography © 2002 Jerry Harpur
Illustrations © 2002 Kate Simunek

Project editor: **Helen Woodhall**
Designer: **Geoff Hayes**
Editorial assistant: **Esme West**
Copy editor: **Sharon Amos**
Picture research: **Esme West and Jess Walton**
Production: **Lorraine Baird & Sha Huxtable**
Index: **Helen Snaith**

A Cataloguing in Publication record for this title is available from the British Library.

Colour separations by Colourscan
Printed and bound by Kyodo

contents

Author's note

I've observed in gardening, as in life, how we all waste time with unnecessary work and make our tasks harder, and often more expensive, with insufficient planning and poor methods. In particular some tasks, such as lawn mowing, weeding and the ritual autumn dig insidiously become unwelcome chores.

My aim is to help remove or reduce the onerous burden of all such potential chores so we can use our garden time for more enjoyable pastimes, such as tending favourite plants, pottering, loafing or whatever you will.

(It's useful to remember something I used to quote when starting a landscape design for a new client: 'I can offer you the choice of a quick job, a cheap job or a proper job: you can even have any two, but never all three together.')

A note on measures

Rather than give conceptually difficult and effectively meaning-lessly precise measurements in metric, I have chosen to go back to a more pragmatic method. As we already adjust so many garden measurements according to the site, soil, variety, convenience and expectation, it is ridiculous to give precise figures. So instead I use nature's natural rulers for all our placing of plants. I use the following indicators: a pace or stride indicates approximately one yard or about one metre; a foot indicates what ever yours is, or about one third your stride; and an inch, or two point five four centimetres if you must, is about as long as the end joint of at least one of your fingers or thumbs; and your longest finger is probably near enough three inches. Obviously if you are very small or very large, compensate for this. Even so, for most of us putting our plants not twelve inches but a real foot apart and not quite three inches but a finger length apart is downright convenient. And you always have the same measure to hand.

1 why make hard work for yourself?

(or how it all went wrong)

If you so wished you could have a perfect bowling green lawn, on any bit of ground, anywhere, no matter how unhopeful it looked. All you have to do is work very diligently and persistently at it, with a very generous budget. But is the effort and expense going to be worth it? Perhaps it may be less stressful to settle for a different, but still quite acceptable, standard of turf and sward rather than to keep striving for a very difficult and almost unachievable mirage.

Now do not get me wrong; if you need the challenge for aesthetic purposes, for exercise or for self development, go ahead. I am all for anyone pursuing whatever is their ideal in gardening, no matter how peculiar. Indeed I perversely keep on trying to grow the difficult or impossible myself. But for the moment and for this book, let us be most concerned with how we can stop making unnecessarily hard work for ourselves. So if you want that pristine bowling green lawn go for it, but do not then dare to whinge on about how much trouble and expense it is taking you.

DON'T ASK THE EXPERTS

I reckon one of the major problems that has beset gardening has been the plethora of artificial and unrealistic standards set by garden designers and the grow-it-for-show exhibitors. Now, of course, the best people to tell us about a subject are usually those who know most about it. If you want a bowling green sward then ask the man who maintains one. But only if you really want that bowling green lawn with all it entails; no heeled shoes, daily cutting, watering, regular feeding, continuous weeding, and strict rolling, aerating and scarifying regimes.

To use an analogy; would you let your granny sign up for her driving lessons with a racing and rallying school or go-cart circuit? All she wants to do is pass her test so she can drive to the supermarket, while on the racetrack they drive with another aim and attitude entirely. Racing drivers can drive safely on the roads, indeed more so because of their extra skills. But your granny has no need to learn hand-brake turns and double de-clutching skills – all these could ever do is confuse the issues for her.

If all we're really after is a bit of soft green turf for the kids to play on or a pleasant path or lawn that needs as little maintenance as possible, the bowling green expert is the last person we should ask. When we ask how to get a nice lawn he tells us, BUT he is after an expert result; his career and reputation rest on it. His vision of what it is we want, what this might entail us doing to get it, the budget required, and what will probably actually be done to make our lawn in the end, are all different pictures. And all of gardening is like this; the experts and their advice are not wrong, just inappropriate. Sure, if you want to grow rare orchids, propagate difficult subjects or grow specimen exhibits for show, then the expert's special skills and knowledge are called for. But they are not the people to ask how to manage the more mundane.

Naturally, once we have gardened for a while it is only to be expected that we might become interested in one area or some group of plants, or even in growing for show and prizes. As an interest becomes a hobby so the amount of information accessed increases and eventually many an enthusiastic amateur becomes very knowledgeable in their field; often exceeding the more acknowledged experts. At this level, especially if show-bench prizes are sought, the labour-intensive methods used by the great gardeners of yesterday can become applicable and even interesting, but to the rest of us these exertions seem just too much effort to consider taking on. While it is true that the more you put in the more you can get out, you must also ask: is it worth it?

GROWING FOR SHOW OR FOR THE TABLE?

When you grow for the table and your own pleasure, one set of methods is applicable; but if you wish to cultivate the more difficult varieties, to win prizes at shows or make a profitable return in cash then the methods must obviously become different. It is as foolish to apply the prize-winner's methods to the average garden as it is to employ amateur methods or tools in a large-scale commercial nursery. Yet we blithely copy the ways of antiquated head gardeners with a dozen underlings, the techniques of the tomato grower who sells tasteless red balls year round and those of the rose expert whose methods resemble an outdated science lesson.

Unfortunately, expert gardeners have made gardening apparently complicated and difficult, with every plant needing its own special treatment and endless lists of tasks and chores for every day of the year. They are not wrong in what they wrote, or still write, but it is inappropriate for most of us. They were, and are, after a different level of perfection, and in the olden days they had fourteen or forty under-gardeners to do the menial tasks. Today the famous vine at Hampton Court still requires a dedicated full-time gardener working for most of the year to produce the magnificent show of superb bunches of

'While it is true that the more you put in the more you can get out, you must also ask: is it worth it?'

grapes hanging like, well, like grapes. Few of us wish to or can spend all our time tending but one plant. But that is effectively what following expert advice leads to.

Below: Well done! What do you do in your spare time?

BIGGER AND BETTER

Whereas we would be glad of a few tasty tomatoes or a couple of bunches of grapes and satisfied just to have a show of roses, the experts want a world where each has an enormous bloom bigger than anyone else's, the grapes crop a hundred bunches to the vine and the tomatoes a hundredweight a square foot. And of course, it is just such experts and their books who have threatened our love for gardening and, in particular, for rose growing. The tragedy of this wonderful flower gets a well-deserved chunk of a chapter to itself later.

The reign of expert gardeners arose along with the creation of rich men's huge walled gardens, and the florist's horticultural shows where compulsive workaholics strove to give each other more employment. The tacit conspiracy between judges and exhibitors has ensured that rarely has a class of entry ever been set that could be won by a keen amateur who grew the usual varieties in his own garden. The winners, and often the judges, of prizes in any class were, and still are, almost invariably from a group of commercial growers in trade with that particular class. It is easy to find six perfect flowers, or twenty-four different perfect ones, if you have a field full of them; harder if you have but a dozen plants.

It would not have been so bad if the shows had encouraged the amateur a little more with their own classes. Some few did, but in general, the displays of massive vegetables and mountains of blooms acted more to dissuade others from competing. Particularly as the means necessary to attain the prizes became less and less like average gardening methods. For example, few prize-winning carrots or parsnips have been grown in the ground for decades. Instead they are grown in barrels and the longest in drainpipes. Leek growers do not start their plants off from seed like the rest of us but vegetatively reproduce their winners from offsets. The blooms of many show flowers have become so huge they need wires to support them.

To go back to a motoring analogy; if you want to compete in Formula 1, you need a Formula 1 car. Your old saloon just will not do, no matter how great your skill. Thus prizes go to show varieties that have been bred, as well as grown, just to show. Now there's nothing wrong with this, but it does lead to confusion. Few people know or grow the contemporary show varieties but are gulled into believing their own plants should perform just as well. Rather like some self-deluded teenage driver wildly imagining his beat-up motor is a Formula 1; no matter how stupid or reckless his driving he will never get his dogmobile to perform like a Ferrari.

You see when we ask the expert how to grow amazing plants like he does, he then tells us. But he tells us how to grow plants exactly like the ones he does – not how to fill the average

> '. . . this is the biggest sin of all – the neglect of flavour and quality in what are essentially food items.'

garden with bloom all summer or how to feed the family, or how to grow gourmet crops. All too often we listen to experts tell us how to do something correct in itself but inappropriate to what we are after. Take tomatoes, for example; the methods the expert market gardener will tell us to use are those that give maximum yield per square yard of covered heated glass year round; while the seeds man will tell us how they produce tomatoes to win prizes at horticultural shows. Neither of which is really very suitable advice for us kitchen gardeners who want to know how we can easily grow reasonably early tomatoes in an unheated domestic greenhouse (with more than their fair share of neglect) and how we can have the best-flavoured fruits.

NEVER MIND HOW THEY LOOK, WHAT DO THEY TASTE LIKE?

At horticultural shows the experts have so much control that few of the fruit and vegetable exhibits actually have to have any residue of taste or nutritional value left at all. Virtually none of any fresh show produce is ever tasted or tested by the judges yet it is given prizes for looking good. It is as insane as if literary

Opposite: Not prize winners but the sweetest fruits: Langley Gage gooseberries.

prizes were awarded solely on the merit of the garishness of the book's bloody cover. (The bird-fancying world is worse – egg-laying backyard fowl varieties are not judged on the size, taste, colour or sheer production of their eggs but on the prettiness of their feathers.)

To my mind this is the biggest sin of all – the neglect of flavour and quality in what are essentially food items. I do not mind if the blooms on show are unreal or unattainable in the average garden but I do object to the way most show produce classes are never tested for their primary purpose. Not only should a display of strawberries look good they should be judged almost entirely on their eating quality. Likewise with potatoes, leeks or cabbage; it is bizarre that they could ever be thought to be judgeable before cooking!

SIZE ISN'T EVERYTHING

This juvenile obsession with size and the neglect of flavour is not a solely British fault, but we have gone to extremes in our competitions. Even trials by the great and the good authorities quoted in gardening magazines give yields and compare appearance but rarely ever mention the taste or cooking quality. For example, if you visit a British leek or gooseberry show do you ever get to taste any leeks or gooseberries, or any delicious dishes made from them? Go to similar shows in many other countries and you find that they are wholehearted celebrations of the culinary versatility of the main exhibits and all around people are consuming the brethren of the show pieces. Thank goodness we now have Apple Days and Potato Days, where some effort is made to recall the true values of these delights.

DOWN ON THE ALLOTMENT

But the pressure for hugeness and uniformity does not stop with the competitive experts; most of us probably have never grown for show yet there was, and still is in some places, a certain degree of 'allotment cred' enforced. You could never be reckoned much of a gardener till you showed off a thirty foot

Opposite: A 'good' show or food on the table?

row of parsnips all equal and equally spaced, the same of beetroot and the same of Brussels sprouts. It did not and does not matter that you didn't care for, or ever ate sprouts, beets or parsnips; you just had to grow them. Which was fortunate, for woe betide you if you took one out of the row, spoiling its perfection and risking the cup on judgement day.

Fortunately the times are changing and now many allotments and gardens are not quite so totalitarian and conformist. Nonetheless there is a tendency to continue doing what's always been done. Indeed too many allotment groups put pressure on their members to have a 'good show' for the judgement day, ignoring the fact that the produce should have long gone to feed the gardener's family while it was at its best and not have been retained to make a neat appearance in unsullied rows. The 'good old boys' advice is often the same as the experts if a touch outdated; they're still aiming for the ludicrousness of big is beautiful and a full row is perfection.

Too many crops are grown as if they were to be shown, or are grown as if they were a commercial crop. These may not be the best methods for the home gardener but we take the advice we were offered and carry on doing the same. Thus we find peas are still sown in a wide flat drill, just so they come up under the wigwam of pea sticks. But this has long been replaced by a strip of netting and now the wide drill makes the peas emerge away from their supports instead of under them.

WHERE DO WE GO FROM HERE?

So where do we turn for good advice? Questions are being asked, by ourselves, the kitchen gardener and the gourmet, and they are not being answered by the many experts whose advice is sincerely offered but commercially biased towards other aims. To be fair, some of the experts could, if pinned down and given time, give appropriate answers to our questions. (One major grower I know admitted with some embarrassment that he never ate his own firm's crops; he had his own plot where he grew the carrots and so on that he and his family consumed.)

In most 'gardening slots' there is never enough time or space to give reasons, options or alternatives. Magazine articles and newspapers are constrained, even books are limited – and a TV programme would have all the knowledge of tomato culture reduced to 'What's the best tom, John?' showing the local garden centre's best plant being popped into a clean pot of virgin compost, then followed by library footage of a ripe crop.

Television programmes are the most misleading as it is so easy for them to cheat. Do not believe all you see, especially the pleasure of those in receipt of a makeover by the experts. (So desperate are we to appear on the silver screen I swear you will find takers for any bizarre offering that guarantees exposure.) TV offers commercialised and crassly simplified advice turned into instant sound bites and pat remarks. It is intended to catch the viewers' attention not to engage with it. Rarely is space allowed to give the full range of advice each and every gardening question poses. Some programmes are hard to tell apart from trade advertisements extolling the virtues of this product or another.

> '. . . instant makeovers have threatened to turn gardening from a relaxing pastime into a physical and stylistical assault course. . .'

Expert presenters who know their stuff deserve their position more than the current 'pretty face' variety, but either should be listened to with caution where they are potentially self serving. In an industry-driven hobby such as gardening, fortunes can be made selling stylish trash to an unwitting public. Ask those people now hemmed in by leylandii hedges taller than their chimney, whose homes are being undermined by the poplar *Populus* x *jackii* 'Aurora', and who will soon be breaking their ankles on slippery decking or flaking blue paint.

Spates of television programmes featuring instant makeovers have threatened to turn gardening from a relaxing pastime into a physical and stylistical assault course and panic attack. Forgetting that 'more haste means less speed'; the 'must be done by five o'clock syndrome' has been foisted onto every gardening slot, together with the promotion of cheating Chelsea cottage gardens and their impressionistic show of unattainable perfection. All this done to make us whip our own more humble plots into some ludicrous sham, and much more importantly,

persuading us to spend more of our cash. (To some extent, fortuitously, fruit and vegetable culture is ignored as there's little money to be made from it.)

Naturally, real gardeners know this instant gardening approach has always led to sore backs, rash decisions, accidents and bodged jobs.

Just look at some of the travesties we have had foisted upon us by those whose trade it is to proffer unattainable dreams – garden designers, often aided by unscrupulous nurserymen with a load of duff stock to unload. Who, for example, ever could have thought roses would make good ground cover? Unbelievable; just try and extricate a weed or a bit of litter from amongst a thriving bed of thorns.

It is painfully obvious that only a few garden designers have ever actually maintained a garden. (At the time of writing at least one popular TV personality garden designer was alleged to not even have a garden!) It is one thing to design a pretty picture garden, especially if it can be falsified at a show such as Chelsea. It is harder by far to make a real one that endures, beautiful in every season and throughout the years and without needing huge amounts of maintenance. This is true on any scale; you can find many gardens, big or small, that are hard work to cope with simply because of their poor design. To say nothing of the dreadful choice of plants so frequently imposed.

Of course there are always reasons that can be given for why things were done that particular way. Economic costs are usually highest on the list, then expediency and quirk seem to follow. But many times I have wondered to myself 'Exactly why did that idiot put that path just there and not along the more obviously convenient route?' And why, if included at all, does the garden shed have to be as inaccessible as possible and the compost heap so remote?

Gardening has been plagued by non-gardening presenters. There was a TV programme on instant gardens that showed how any half handy bodger could turn a pleasant garden into an al fresco living space (otherwise known as a patio) with wooden decking, weird chairs and a garish paint job. Of course they showed the immediate effect and not the result after a couple of wet summers in Britain's mouldy climate, when the decking slimes over and turns into a death trap and the paint festers and peels. It was not that gaily painted decking was wrong; just inappropriate. It would have been nice in Nice or Cannes but really not suited to damp old Blighty.

And this is the major problem; inappropriateness. The experts and professionals are in good faith (let us be charitable), but they are providing answers to the questions they think we are asking and not giving us the information we need for our own more pragmatic ends. And truly there is never one answer to any given gardening question but many. How then is the novice, or even the old hand, going to decide which to follow? Well, I hope this book will help you, as the old coach always said, to keep your eye on the ball...

Below: Nice in Nice or Cannes but in Blighty? Note the high-tide marks on the seats (perches) and table bases!

2 ways to save work

NOT ALL TASKS ARE NECESSARY

We have inherited a gardening culture aspiring to unattainable perfection, which dictates that we must do this and that or dire results will occur. Luckily for us, and our plants, most of gardening is common sense and we need only remember that left to themselves, seeds germinate and plants grow, flower and fruit, that is their nature.

Obviously, there are a few things that are foolish beyond belief in terms of making work and these are usually made in the planning stage. For example, never put a beech hedge next to a patio: beech leaves drop over half the year making it necessary to continually sweep them up. Likewise, it may be aesthetically pleasing to have a large number of small beds separated by grass paths, but the amount of regular edging required is excessive, the mowing difficult and the effect piecemeal. Far better to have fewer bigger bolder beds, with fewer edges to neaten.

Another way to cut out work is to stop doing totally unnecessary things. You may see some folks tying up their daffodil leaves in neat little bundles once the flowers have died. This is totally counter-productive labour; the leaves need to be spread in the sun until they have withered away, which is at least six weeks after flowering finishes. It's just another make-work scheme from the Victorian high gardening era that continues mindlessly on. The same can be said for the regular autumn digging over of the garden; this is almost a total waste of effort as I shall show in a later chapter, as is the collecting and burning of leaves and almost all the rigmarole of recommendations for lawn care.

Another important way to reduce work is to give up chores that give little in return for their effort. Some tasks can hardly be avoided, such as sowing seeds, but you never need thin them if you don't sow too thickly in the first place. After all, why sow five hundred parsnip seeds per yard if all you want are half a dozen plants there in a few weeks time?

Some work is really not worth the effort; onions for example need several effective weeding sessions when they're small, but it's actually counter-productive to continue to weed them later when they're maturing. Likewise, many people cut their hedges twice when once would have sufficed if the timing was spot on, or if excessive fertiliser hadn't been applied.... So much of conventional advice is designed to ensure the heaviest possible crops, but if massive yields are not important to you then much of this extra work can be curtailed, especially regarding applications of chemical fertilisers whose use often causes problems later.

I have grown almost every type of fruit and vegetable, and designed AND maintained dozens of gardens and I reckon it's easy to cut back the labour required with some jobs if you do other jobs better. For example, a good mulch properly applied reduces weeding and watering requirements significantly; prompter pruning in summer and winter prevents the spread and build up of pests and diseases, saving much effort later.

Grouting a crazy-paving path thoroughly will leave no place for a weed to get hold. Likewise it is little use hoeing away at weeds and cursing at their multitudes if you let other ones seed away freely nearby. Everything in the garden is interconnected and it really does pay to do each job as well as you can. Not only is it more satisfying but it saves so much otherwise wasted time when you have to re-do it later.

An old carpenter told me the best gardening advice I ever heard: 'Think each job out at least thrice, measure up at least twice and then do it but once, properly!'

Below: Don't buy now; get these in autumn so they flower in your garden rather than perish there.

CAPITAL VS CASH; GOOD TOOLS

One of the biggest problems facing most gardeners is a shortage of funds. Everything is easier with more cash. Professional tools can be employed instead of poor quality ones sold to the unwitting novice. You need only a few tools so get really good ones; secondhand tools are often of a far better quality than modern manufactured ones, especially trowels and hoes, and possibly mowers. Good tools hold an edge and stay sharp, cutting more cleanly with less effort. It is false economy to buy cheap tools, particularly secateurs or hoes, as these are so important and used so often. Likewise if you need a barrow,

> **'Good tools hold an edge and stay sharp, cutting cleanly with less effort.'**

then buy a good one that will last such as a builder's barrow and not some stylish plastic travesty with multicoloured wheels. Tasks are made easier by having the right tool so moving hay, straw or muck is much less effort if you have a muck fork with wide-spaced strongly curved tines. But ask yourself first if you need one.

Conserve your capital by not buying gadgets and gizmos or complicated tools you will rarely use, such as hedge trimmers, chain saws or rotary cultivators. It will be cheaper to rent these for the day or so when they're needed, rather than to have them sitting around all year only to take a half day to get started. An engine, particularly a two stroke, that is rarely used can be a b****** to get going – it really can take longer than the trip to the hire shop – believe me.

But is a specialised power tool really necessary? Do you need to fetch and carry some beast of a machine that belches pollution in your face? (And seen realistically, the electric one is no better as you still get the pollution on the wind from the power station.) Do not believe the blandishments of the adverts; cutting a big hedge is never going to be easy no matter how powerful your trimmer and how butch its name. I have gone back to the safer, quieter, use of a pair of shears. Sure, it takes longer but it is nicer work and nowhere near as arduous. I am not trying to cut my hedge as economically as possible but in as stress free a way as possible, and wielding a motorised tree axe is just not nice.

The same applies to much mechanised gardening; it may be quicker but it may not be pleasanter or even easier. Don't forget – everyone wants to sell you something expensive rather than something cheaper that would do instead. I have been very impressed by nylon-line trimmers; they are amazing for quickly tidying rough areas and trimming shrubs, hedges, lawns and edges. Marvellous, but noisy and they damage bark and fling stones. The perfect tool for a commercial gardener with a job to get done in short time, but back here at home I use a hand-held reap hook to do just the same jobs if a bit more slowly – and I can hear the birds sing while I work.

So save money on the hardware but do not economise on the plants – except possibly to buy fewer of them. It is rarely ever a good buy to purchase a cheap plant. If it is cheap because it is easy to propagate, such as lavender, blackcurrant or rosemary you would get a better plant for free by rooting a cutting yourself. If it is difficult to root, needs grafting or is rare, then why is this specimen cheap? Beware, cheapness is not a good sign. The plant may be diseased or pest-ridden, too old and root bound and cramped in too small a pot. Lost label, end of line and other such lures are a waste of money as the plant is unlikely to be a choice one for which you have been searching.

Buy from a reputable nursery who grow much of their own stock. Look around; is it just a retail site or are they actually growing anything (other than richer)? And don't buy big plants but small ones; a smaller plant will often establish quicker and soon outgrow a larger specimen put in at the same time. And if you want several ask for a discount, and if you want loads, say for a hedge, then think about propagating them yourself. A little planning can save a great deal of cash as well as work.

Opposite: A good pair of secateurs is a useful investment.

OVERPRODUCTION IS THE USUAL RESULT IF PLANTS GROW AT ALL

One of the ironies of gardening is that much of the information given is to increase yields at the margin when, in fact, most years result in glut or famine depending on the weather. With most crop plants there is a minimum amount of care, rain and sun required, and given these, you end up giving away bags of surplus. If care, rain or sun are lacking then you starve....

Most of the battle is getting the plants established, from then on they respond generously. With runner beans, for example, most of the difficulty is getting them to germinate and grow away in a cold year. Yet most books talk about putting a trench full of compost under the seeds to provide moisture for a bigger crop. Talk about making work: any problem with runner beans is in the early stages; they crop only too heavily once they get big enough. Indeed they usually crop so well they are casually given away by the bag freely to all comers.

The same goes for tomatoes. These plants are going to set a crop regardless and unless you do something really bad, such as leave them in tiny pots, they are going to produce a big crop if they have plenty of soil and water, but they will only ripen into a sweet crop if there is also plenty of sun. That's it; everything else you can do is inconsequential by comparison. Giving them too much feed when there is too little sun causes problems itself.

EYE ON THE BALL: TOMATOES NOT TOMATO PLANTS

A neighbour visited my garden one sunny summer day and while wandering past the greenhouse he remarked how awful my tomatoes looked. I was hurt and asked him to explain what he thought wrong. His reasoning was that my plants were spindly, with small hard leaves and the trusses had few ripe fruits on them. He then took me to see his; tropical jungle was the impression that hit me as he slid open the door to his greenhouse. I couldn't see anything for the enormous leaves on the gigantic dark green vines filling the whole space. Where are the tomatoes I asked? He shoved aside an armful of leaves to show a massive truss of great big green billiard balls. I was impressed with how much weight he got per plant and asked what they tasted like. Taste! He hadn't had one ripen yet; he reckoned he would get them ripening in a month's time.

I pointed out the reason my plants had few tomatoes on per truss was because I had been eating mine for two months already even though I had no more heat in my greenhouse than did he. His problem was that he was growing tomato plants not tomatoes. You don't eat big leaves but ripe fruits, yet he was feeding and fertilising like a commercial grower who would be cropping the plants for far longer in his commercial greenhouse. My neighbour's expenditure on fertiliser was increasing his yield but it was also setting back the ripening of the crop. And at the end of his short season yet another box of surplus tomatoes was not a lot of compensation for having none earlier.

If your idea of heaven is showing off a greenhouse full of immaculate tomato plants replete with massive trusses of pumped-up fruits then you need to approach the task differently to the person who wants to eat decent-tasting tomatoes over as many months as possible, as cheaply as possible. The hardest task in gardening is deciding what it is you want; once that's done the ends to achieve it are usually straightforward and obvious. But you must also decide what you don't want and get rid of it. Do not persist with weeding a tiny little border that has no great value just because it's there. Grass it over and make another border or bed bigger instead. Don't put up with ducking and diving to avoid a low branch; chop it off and make your task easier.

HAVE FEWER WASTED PLANTS

It is far better to have fewer plants and then there will be fewer wasted hours. Invariably, whether in the vegetable or flower garden, the fewer the plants grown the better they are grown. Given the same space, a few plants fill it just as do many. Too many plants will need to compete and none of them can become as magnificent a specimen as when growing among less competition. Over-crowding from more of the same is as bad or worse than the competition from weeds. Do not go to the effort of germinating a hundred seeds, pricking out six dozen seedlings and potting up three dozen plants if all you want are six! I cannot believe the surplus seedlings and plants that we spend time and effort on that are never used. Exactly how many Brussels sprout plants did you really need?

DO NOT TAKE ON TOO MUCH. GROW A FEW WELL

Where a multitude of different sorts of plant is grown there is a tendency for us to apply a uniform method of care. Thus many survive but few prosper. Whereas if a gardener grows only a few choice favourites the more individual attention they receive will make them flourish. The same applies in every situation but especially where saving work is the priority.

Plants indoors in pots need careful and regular watering. If you have many or few you condemn yourself to a frequent round with the watering can. And what for? In many homes, I'll bet most house plants are in need of re-potting, feeding, more water, light or a warmer situation. It is going to impress more visitors to have half a dozen wonderful house plants than to have every surface crammed with choked and dying travesties. Equally, outdoors in the flower garden and the orchard, an encyclopaedic collection of every sort will rarely impress as much as a damn fine show of a few excellent specimens.

There is unfortunately a tendency to take on too much; to have grand schemes and then to fail to keep up with them. Far better to keep the largest part simple and show off all your skill in one or two special areas that are really important to you.

And likewise with space; near enough the same produce or effect can be had from a small space as from a large one, depending on how you approach it and how you keep up with it. I've seen so many people worn down by the effort of keeping up with a whole allotment when a half or even a quarter share would have served better. It is easy enough to mark out and dig over a nice new bed or border; it's another thing to keep up with the weeding when it turns green overnight with a billion seedlings everywhere, including in amongst your treasured plants.

The old hands have the advantage of knowing just what they can get away with, and know that it's easier running a garden than it is getting it up and started. And of course many of us are dropped in it when we move house and have to start straightaway. Then it pays to concentrate on keeping up those parts that are already in good shape AND IGNORING any area that is already derelict – except for cutting down weed seed heads and areas near the house for access. Don't take on restoring it all at once.

Below: Small-fruited tomatoes are more reliable croppers than the more impressive larger ones.

Above: Why have lawn when this is prettier and easier to maintain?

SPECIALISE. MY CHOICE PLANTS ARE EDIBLE, SCENTED OR APHRODISIAC

To a novice all of gardening is new and some aspects seem immediately more appealing. As interest broadens, other areas become interesting that at first seemed barren. For example, initially you may be taken by large bold flowers such as gladioli, or repulsed by them. Later you may change your opinion, even becoming besotted by plants without flowers at all. Read any sort of book on gardening but actually practise on only a few things to start with. As I've said already, concentrate on just a few plants to grow very well with all your attention. As your skill improves other plants that are more difficult can be taken on.

Even though I have a lot of space, nearly an acre, I laid down a rule for my garden that I wouldn't grow anything unless it was edible or scented (or aphrodisiac – for to quote Milton: 'hope springs eternal...') and my ideal is a plant that's all three. There just is not room for every plant I take a fancy to, so at least by applying this rule I can keep the numbers down somewhat. You can be as ruthless as you like; making a garden of just white

flowers or green flowers may be hard but actually may well be less work than the usual garden because you only have one aim to fulfil.

GROW WHAT GROWS WELL AND EASILY LOCALLY

If you wish to be known as a really good gardener, do not try to fight nature but go with her. For the bulk of your plantings, grow what does well naturally in your area on your soil. Walk around your neighbourhood every few weeks and note which flowers and shrubs, which fruits and which vegetables always seem to look good in other people's gardens. A derelict garden also offers many informative signs. Any plant that is thriving and putting on a good show in a derelict garden is getting exactly the amount of work applied to it we want to be aiming for.

Here are lessons for us; those plants in nearby gardens that have nothing done to them and put on a good show are at least known to do well with no work and give an indication of their size in your soil and situation. If you want them to do even better, just give them a little more space when you grow them. If there are a lot of happy-looking hydrangeas or hollies, carrots, cabbages or even date palms in your area then grow those. But plant them small, give them plenty of space, a well dug and generous hole, good soil conditions with a thick mulch and plentiful water and you will grow magnificent specimens. Grow your favourites as well but make the bulk of your plantings from those things that flourish naturally in your locality and you will have far more show for far less work. I live in East Anglia, a bit of the UK that is dry in summer, with a thin limy soil, in a frost pocket prone to winter flooding; it is hardly surprising that I fail to keep choice delights such as daphnes and blueberries alive for long. I can only dream of rhododendrons (well I wouldn't want most of them anyway, except a few of the scented ones, and then only in pots), but my cabbages and cherries are fantastic. Funnily enough the watermelon crop never seems very big, though....

Opposite: In a very little time this greenhouse will be a dark shed unless the honeysuckle is moved to climb a tree instead.

ALWAYS CHOOSE THE RIGHT TIME IN GARDENING

This may be true for most things but particularly so with gardening where you do not have control of many factors such as the weather. The plants and the seasons can not be hurried. Indeed much of the secret of successfully effortless gardening is in the timing. The old adage is that 'the difference between a good gardener and a bad one is a fortnight'; another says 'there is no time like the right time and the right time was last month'.

I once watched new neighbours move in during a hot spell. While I enjoyed the brief respite from hard work early summer brings, these keen folk set to with the intention of clearing their overgrown garden. They cut down the verdant stand of nettles, brambles, docks and grasses as tall as your head and for a week pulled out a skip load of bits of wire and brick and bottles etc. Then they tried to level the rough ground which was now dried out and as hard as a brick, bound tight with the roots of all the weeds.

If they had just waited. First they could have enjoyed the natural beauty of the lush growth as it was because for sure it was not pretty after they had cleared it. Instead they should have waited till mid winter when all the leaves were off the brambles and the nettles had died down. Then they could have picked up the debris, removed wire and basically cleared the growths and junk above ground much more easily.

In winter, the ground is softer and easier to dig, cultivate or move and the roots of tough weeds can be pulled out. Or a cleared area can be left and simply cut with a rough mower once growth commences in spring; it will soon appear neat and become quite a good sward as the year progresses. All the brambles, nettles and weeds will be chopped by the mower and turned into fertility; but more on that later in this book.

Another example of waiting for the right time to make less work is hammering in posts or digging holes. It is very hard work to knock in a post in the dry soil of late spring and summer; it is much easier in the soft soil of late autumn and winter. And digging holes in dry ground is very slow and hard, so at least moisten it well the day before if you can't wait till the right season.

On the other hand, there is that old saying about a stitch in time and this certainly applies to pest and disease control, where letting any attack proceed on vulnerable plants can be risky. (Established plants can be left to endure conditions much less favourable than the small, newly sown or planted, and those in pots and under cover.) Likewise prompt action is required with weeds among young plants – they should never be allowed to establish and seed. A few weeds setting seed guarantees seven years more weeding.

Work done quickly and promptly does save so much wasted time. A fine example is a sticking latch on the garden gate or the shed. Say you have to fiddle with it for a couple of seconds to get it to work at all instead of properly and promptly. Now suppose you go to that shed or gate just a couple of times a day. Over a year the time accumulates and just those two seconds twice a day is over twenty-four minutes a year wasted wrestling with the catch. If you use it four times a day or it sticks a little longer then you will be spending a whole hour fiddling with the damn thing. So why not get the tools and fix it now before it steals any more of your precious time.

In gardening one of the biggest makers of work and wasters of time is the grass which I reckon needs cutting about thirty times in a year. With this the hours of wasted effort and hard work soon mount up, so I will deal with it straight away.

Opposite: Sit down and think the job out first.

3

make mowing easier

Mowing the lawn is one of the most time-consuming tasks in the garden. For a neat lawn you really need to cut it frequently. In moist climates it needs a cut every week during the growing season, with just a cut every other week or so in late autumn and early spring. Even with time off for a browned-out lawn lasting a fortnight or two each summer, I reckon many of us must do at least thirty cuts or more a year. Because of the large number of times the grass must be cut it is essential to make each trim as short as possible (without then making it too hard). Just two minutes wasted by bad planning each time you cut adds up to an hour a year: if you can knock twenty minutes off each cut, that's ten hours of the hardest work you've saved every year.

Of course, as I've said, 'If you like the exercise...' but if you are serious about trying to save unnecessary work in your garden, look at your time spent mowing. As heretical as this may seem, it may be worth paying someone to cut the grass for you, so you can have time to do the more enjoyable gardening tasks. Admittedly it does risk your garden's well-being if you get a poor workman who is careless with your mower. But this of all gardening jobs is one that is fairly easy to delegate. 'Cut the grass' is pretty difficult to misunderstand. Whether you can find anyone willing, capable, affordable and reliable, is another matter.

Then anyway one has to ask whether having a lawn or grassed path is appropriate? An emerald green sward is a beautiful foil for flowers and foliage, but does it take up a disproportionate amount of effort to maintain? If you don't have much space, it makes a lot of sense to dispense with any grass altogether and to have the areas nearest the house as hard-standing patio. As you get further away, both the beds and the paths can be mulched with pebbles or bark. It is least work to have paths of slabs and stepping stones set into a thick mulch. This means you can get rid of the lawnmower and the edge trimmers, freeing up storage space as well as saving a lot of work. True you now have more ground to keep weed free, but mulches will do that for you. And there will no longer be grass and other weeds creeping in from the sward to the beds.

In a larger garden the areas become too large to pave or mulch and it becomes an economic necessity to have turf paths, lawns and even wilder grassed areas such as orchards. But we do not really need to maintain them as bowling greens; grass maintenance has been dominated for too long by experts who look after the bowling green, the golf range and the football pitch. Though to be fair the last has to deal with almost the same problems as the gardener in a house with small children.

Above: This feature would look more inviting beside a path rather than tacked on the side of the lawn, save mowing and put a big bed in the left-hand foreground!

THE WRONG EXPERTS WITH THE WRONG SWARD

A story tells of the tourist who asked a famous college's gardener how he got the lawns so perfect and was told you just cut and rolled and fed and watered for about four hundred years or so. Absolutely correct, and good advice if you can follow it. And the so-called experts have been after much the same result but want it quicker, and have then caused themselves and us problems and more work in the process. They speak of inordinate amounts of raking, aerating, scarifying and scratching, working in top dressings and lawn sands, rolling and ever more frequent cuts.

The experts' situations are specialised: the bowling or golf green is a demanding place with but one use. The sward's existence revolves around its performance. Even its grasses are not as ours...

Its turf is composed of very fine-bladed grasses that make a fine brush-like sward. Unfortunately, these fine grasses need an acid soil to survive. As do the most pernicious weeds. These 'fine' grasses are also the most expensive grass seeds sold to us as 'the best' by every seed supplier.

In fact, what most of us really want are the far cheaper, more vigorous tough grasses that will take some damage and neglect, and still look good. These timothy and ryegrass mixtures are offered for shady and hard-wearing areas. They would be little good for the expert's purposes; but the experts have no unwanted shade from the neighbour's house to contend with, and they are not going to let anyone wearing high heels walk on their bowling green or play football on their golf range.

> '. . . grass maintenance has been dominated for too long by the experts who look after the bowling green...'

SWARD CARE AND CONTROLLING TURF WEEDS

Now the grasses the experts ignore are tougher, more vigorous species that mostly prefer alkaline conditions – just the sort of soils you find in most gardens. This is important as it means we can use lime, which the experts cannot, on their acid-loving swards. This gives an advantage to clover and grasses while discouraging weeds such as the speedwell veronicas. These are difficult weeds to control, even with chemicals, and plague most grass lawns as they thrive in acid conditions, but they do not like regular dustings of lime.

Lime sweetens the topmost layer of soil among the grasses' roots; even in a chalky soil this layer can become acidic as thatch (a mesh of partly decayed grass leaves) and detritus build up. By liming this layer, the common grass weeds such as veronicas and mosses are discouraged while simultaneously the more alkaline soil encourages clovers. On most soils a handful of finely ground chalk limestone per square yard or metre sprinkled on in winter makes a good annual dressing. On acid soil and old sward use up to four handfuls.

Now although sward experts strive to maintain a perfect monoculture of fine grasses in their turf, this is not actually necessary. Clover is seen by them as a weed to be eradicated, rather than a companion providing fertility and keeping the lawn greener in dry periods. I have often been asked: 'How do you get rid of those green patches in the lawn when it all goes khaki coloured in a drought?' The answer is to sow clover everywhere else. Clover attracts more dew and is leguminous, which means it provides free nitrogen to the grasses growing with it. The more luxuriant growth of clover and grass then suppresses the weeds. On many soils in the UK white or Dutch clover (*Trifolium repens*) is a common weed, but it is the best clover to over-sow in spring into a sward as it is prostrate and very low growing. Crimson and red clovers are also attractive but are taller growing and less suitable.

Conventional advice was also intended to make the grass flourish but by applying the horticultural equivalent of anabolic steroids. Grass was said to need regular stimulation with a host of chemical fertilisers: these certainly made the grass flourish initially and go a lush dark green – where it didn't go brown from an overdose. The problems were unseen but frequent use of soluble chemical fertilisers was killing off the natural fertility-forming organisms in the soil. This made the soil poorer and, worse, it killed the worms.

Above: Clover provides free fertiliser for your grass.

But the conventional advice was to discourage worms anyway; they were considered a pest. They were killed with chemicals deliberately, inadvertently by the acidification of the soil, and also by the use of moss killers and other chemicals. Their casts were seen as a problem and so the worms were destroyed wholesale. Which was short-sighted and foolish; their burrowing had maintained the soil structure, drainage and aeration for millennia. As they were killed off the soil structure degraded and the turf suffered, drying out more in summer and water logging in winter. The more the experts flogged their soil, the more they had to do to maintain it at all.

Chemical fertilisers make the soil acid to enable the 'fine' grasses to flourish. Worms like an alkaline soil so leave or die where much fertiliser is used. Worms need a dressing of lime, and like occasional feeding with blood, fish and bone meal (at a handful or so per square yard or metre in mid spring), or seaweed meal if you prefer, which will also feed the grass but gently and without acidification. These feeds give the worms protein so they breed; more worms means more aeration and drainage, more minerals brought up from deep down. Their efforts make a richer turf for us and save us most of the allegedly necessary work of the lawn-care experts.

Growing tough lime-loving grasses also helps get rid of daisies. Daisies have a very high need for calcium and are very competitive for it, more so than grass. If you see daisies proliferating while the grass pales, it is a fair bet the soil is getting short of lime. Daisies also prosper when the grass is cut too short and are choked out if the grass is cut a bit higher.

The most annoying lawn weeds are the rosette type, such as thistles, dandelions and plantains. These can be easily grubbed up with a knife but it is tiresome work and they tend to regrow.

The old-fashioned thistle-pulling tool that pulls them up with a wee forked end rotated on a pivot works wonders but these tools are hard to find. So, although it is politically incorrect, where local laws allow it, I suggest you try child labour. Put them on a piece rate and pay generously – you might even make a profit from their parents for occupying them for a while. Given an old blunt knife and a bucket each, a couple of kids can eliminate all your rosette weeds while you sit in a chair making sure they come to no harm. It is more enticing to say you want to gather these mineral-containing plants to make a 'magic' potion for some secret purpose. (True, they rot down to make a great liquid feed.) Telling the children you just want the lawn cleared of weeds is not as good, believe me.

Below: A handful of lime encourages a healthy sward.

GRASS CUTTING: THE THEORY AND PRACTICE

Not only have the experts caused problems with their abuse of chemicals, they have also made us cut our lawns too short. Now you may want a green fuzz as close cropped as a peach to play bowls or golf on, but as a green backdrop to the flowers, to support a deck chair or a goal post it's not necessary. It is counter-productive: short blades of grass do not exclude the light from all of the soil, giving opportunity for weeds and mosses to grow. Worse, short blades of grass cause the roots to be short and the grass dries out more in droughts. By leaving the blade of grass longer, the plant makes the roots longer and deeper, and the longer blades collect more dew. To have a good sward you must cut as often, but set the blades higher.

Some allegedly labour-saving mowers shred the clippings finely and return them to the sward. Unfortunately, this makes the turf thatchy. Clippings are best collected when bulky, although light amounts and those from the first few and last few cuts are always best scattered onto the sward to feed the worms.

Do not wait till the mower is choked with clippings before emptying it; this reduces its efficiency and makes for more work unblocking the clogged-up jammed machine. Have a barrow or a dustbin or a plastic sheet at either end of long rows or by each area of grass, so you can quickly unload the clippings and move them elsewhere all together later.

To minimise the work disposing of the clippings I use them as a mulch around trees, shrubs, roses and even amongst some vegetables. After all, you've got to put them somewhere so you might as well put them where they'll do some good. Applied in thin layers, they do not form a thick, claggy, smelly mess but a dry cardboard-like mulch – if the birds don't mix them up that is. Applied every week through the growing season, a regularly

Above: Grass clippings make good mulch around the base of plants.

by loads of worm casts. The worms pull the clippings into their runs to digest them, thus another way to get rid of clippings and to get free fertility is to sprinkle them over any soil, anywhere – the worms will find them.

If you do let your grass get away and grow too long, cut it as soon as possible, but late in the day so it is as dry as it can get. Do not try and cut it down all in one pass; cut the grass with the mower set high. Do not cut with the full width of the blades but cut with just half the width biting into new grass and the other half running over the strip already cut. This will be quicker and less work than chewing at a full-width cut. Most mowers can cut the grass but are limited in their ability to move it through in quantity. That's why it's better to take a half-width cut; there is half as much grass to cut and more air is sucked through to help speed it. Likewise, if the grass is drier it weighs less and is easier to move through the machine. If necessary spray the clippings back onto the ground: most machines work better when passing the cuttings through than when collecting them. Allow the cuttings to wither in place then either rake them up, or mow and collect them, or strew them with a second and third cut. Three or so cuts at reducing heights will usually get most overgrown lawns back under control, but they will be patchy especially if long neglected. Don't worry; just cut regularly and

> **'for almost every garden sward a rotary-bladed mower is the most sensible choice.'**

topped-up grass-clipping mulch will suppress almost all weeds. In winter the grass clipping mulch will disappear, to be replaced eventually the bald areas will green over. You can speed the process and improve any poor sward by broadcasting vigorous grass seed over it in spring and autumn. But just regular cutting from the start of the year will convert almost any flat area of weeds into quite a respectable sward from a distance. (Close inspection will reveal all manner of plants surviving, but who cares as long as it looks green and flat.)

CHOICE OF MACHINES, PLUS TRIMMERS

If saving work is no concern and you want to be fit and ecologically pure, get a push mower – you'll feel virtuous and sleep well. For the rest of us, the most important point with a mower is easy starting. It is no good having a mower that takes ages to start and makes you sweaty and upset before you have even got going. Electric mowers have the advantage here but are gutless things otherwise, and you have to haul the cable in and out.

Unfortunately, petrol engines are temperamental. I had a neighbour once who used to cut his lawn after Sunday lunch – just when I'm settling down to listen to myself on BBC Radio Four's *Gardener's Question Time*. Well, the programme used to last half an hour, which was about how long it took my neighbour to cut his grass. However I noticed as the summer went by that although he got the mower out of the shed at the same time each Sunday, he started mowing later and later. He obviously economised on overhauls and spark plugs as the blessed machine became more and more reluctant to get going. Eventually it was taking as much time, and swearing, to get it going as the actual cutting took. And then it over-revved as the blades were worn down.

It's no good persisting with worn blades; if you want your mower to work well and easily and give a good finish then simply change the blades more often. A new set of sharp blades will make an old machine cut like new. Worn blades weigh less and this causes most machines to automatically speed up, leading to more wear on the engine, the bearings and your ears. Worn blades make hard work and cost money so replace yours NOW!

Your choice of machine can make it much harder or easier work for you. It's not just a question of whether or not your mower propels itself but also how easy it is to use, especially to steer in confined spaces. And ride-ons are not less work: instead of a relaxed walk behind, now you have to be bounced up and down and dragged under branches. For the bigger garden I suppose there is some sense to ride-ons but they generally give a poor finish. For the rest of us with only a small lawn and a few paths to cut then the type of machine is more crucial.

There is little point getting a cylinder mower (as used on bowling greens) unless you have a first rate turf; for almost every garden sward a rotary-bladed mower is the most sensible choice. Extra power is always worthwhile, as it means you can cut more easily in wet conditions when the going is heavy. A wider cut means you can mow the same area in fewer passes and it is always worth getting a wider machine. A roller on the back spreads the load better than wheels and gives those silly stripes we all love. Easy clipping removal of the hod or bag is an important point: if it's difficult it will hurt your back as you have to empty it so many times in a year.

A nylon-line trimmer is a useful tool for the professional, but I wouldn't bother with one in a small garden as the same work can be done with a reap hook or pair of shears. Trimmers suffer from the same vices as mowers, if anything more so, particularly

Below: Overhanging lavender reduces the work of neatening the edges of a grass path.

as they usually have two-stroke motors. Nonetheless for the big garden or anyone with a wild area a trimmer is handy. You can trim around the trunks of trees, posts, pedestals, seats etc., making the grass cutting itself more simple and thus easier. Trimmers are also handy for removing weeds growing up out of other plants, for example, nettles and for rough cutting hedges and cutting back flower heads on lavender. They are the quickest way to bring some order into an overgrown garden but are not pleasant work. The engines are noisy, the bits fly around and you chop wildlife into a purée. The smaller petrol or heavier duty electric ones are handy tools, but do not be gulled into buying some laser-guided anti-tank brush cutter that will cut through a telegraph post in milliseconds and needs a harness of straps to carry it. This sort of thing is used by farmers and professionals; what you want is a small lightweight machine you can use without suffering too many pulled muscles. If the job requires a big machine then hire one, with an operator.

EDGING AND HOW TO REDUCE IT

Along with mowing, a great deal of work and time goes on keeping the edges of a grass path or lawn neat. As with everything else a lot can be done to make less work by careful planning. Every piece of edge requires labour regularly, so the less edging the less work. By amalgamating beds and borders whole lengths of edge can be dispensed with. A common opportunity to eliminate some edges occurs where a grass path leads from the patio to the lawn, passing between two beds. Not only will this path always be worn in the middle but, by replacing it with stepping stones or slabs, it makes the two beds into one visually and, more importantly, saves loads of work edging.

Making beds up to existing hard edges such as paths and drives can further reduce edging. For example, it may look nice but a long narrow strip of grass between a long border and a concrete drive is just a make-work scheme. Get rid of it and replace it with low-growing plants such as thymes, which won't impinge on the drive. Alternatively plant the leading edge of the beds and borders with strong, low-growing plants such as lavender, cotton lavender, day lilies and so on. If these are allowed to straggle and hang over the nominal edge you can't see it and border and lawn or path merge seamlessly and without work. However you must be sure your mower will slip cleanly under the overhanging plants without too much snagging or you can't get away with this fudge.

Having reduced the amount of edging to a minimum you could apply a wooden or metal permanent edge. Though somewhat naff they reduce the need to trim regularly. (Absolute foolishness is using upended bricks, tiles, or the height of folly, bottles, as edges. The broken-off bits are unsightly and dangerous while the effect is ghastly and laborious to keep neat.) To trim edges a pair of sharp long-handled edge trimmers is cheap enough, does a good job and is much easier than trying to use ordinary shears. Edges need doing at least fortnightly during the spring and early summer months – you can ease off in autumn. I use a hot-air gun to 'cook' the edges every month or so and this keeps them neat for longer as it kills

Left: Catnip overhanging the edges of a grass path reduces the need for neatening its edges.

Above: Stepping stones save wearing a bare patch down the middle of a grass path.

the leaves. (I used to use my nylon-line trimmer to do the edges; once flat wise then again backwards to do the vertical face. Goodness, it was quick but I gave it up as it took too long to repair the windows broken by flying stones.)

PLANNING PATHS: REMOVING OBSTACLES AND IRRITATIONS

There is an old saying that it takes no talent to be uncomfortable. I had a tall friend once who had a terrible-looking scabby patch on the top of his head. I was so concerned that one day I broached the subject of ozone holes and skin tumours. Tumour be damned, he ranted, it was nothing more than that he kept knocking off the scab every time he cut his grass. The branch of an old tree had fallen over to an angle after a storm some years before. As the branch crossed a path my friend tried to limbo under it as he mowed but often failed to duck sufficiently. The look of relief on his face when I sawed that branch off...

In a similar vein I once had a client who had acquired a patio bounded by a lawn on all sides, which led onto one big border beyond. A nice simple plan with but one bit of grass to cut – simple except for the scalloped edge up against the border. In and out the edge wove so as you tried to mow you had to heave the machine this way and that till your back protested and you almost got seasick. And you couldn't even see those scallops from the patio. By making them into one sweeping curve the mowing time was halved and the effort quartered.

Similarly, any little awkward corner where you have to heave the mower in and out; be done with it. A path that leads nowhere and requires exactly two and a half passes to cut it? Make it narrower and save a wasted journey and a half. Do you have to carefully avoid a stump or a pit in the ground? For goodness sake put it right.

And make sure it's easy to get the mower in and out of the shed. I knew a man once who every week damn near killed himself just extricating the mower from among his tools and then lowering it down three concrete steps.

Do not ever listen to the daft idiot who tells you the best way to repair a worn patch of turf is to use little pieces cut from the edges so that it matches the rest rather than sowing seed there. What he doesn't think about is why is that patch worn? Surely

Above: Green lawnmowers.

once it is repaired it will wear again. And need repairing again, and again. If a patch wears, set a stepping-stone slab into the spot and you'll never need do another repair again.

One grass path I used constantly was going bald up the middle, so I started to walk up one side and down the other, but still it wore. The traffic was too great but the distance too far to afford to pave all the way. So I compromised; I laid one row of slabs corner to corner down the middle. Now I have a hard running surface for the barrow all the way at the minimum cost. I can walk on the slabs, saving wear on the grass and wet feet, and there is no longer a bald patch to repair. And into the bargain the slabs set into the path shoot off the rainfall, making it available to the grass sward on either side. This keeps the sides of the path greener and lusher without my making any effort to water them. Water is also conserved underneath the slabs. Each slab acts as an impermeable mulch and doesn't allow water to evaporate. These water-saving features of slabs and stepping stones are equally labour-saving when they are placed in beds and borders. A simple tip: if your stepping stones or slabs or patio become green and slippery, throw down a little sharp sand. This gives a better grip and the sand wears away the slime – unfortunately the sand can carry indoors on shoes.

> 'It was the search for sweet sounds of wildlife that led me to remake my garden quite profoundly.'

GRADED CUTTING

Apart from giving up entirely or going over to meadow gardening, you can keep grassed areas neat without them all being cut incredibly short. Obviously the grass nearest the house needs be cut most closely and most often but, as you get further away, you can cut less closely and less often. Providing your mower is strong enough, you can get away with cutting once every ten days or so in late spring and early summer and even further apart the rest of the year. Another way is to cut only the central strip of each path and the middle area of the lawn most often and raise the height of the cut, and the time taken between cuts, for the sides and perimeter from the spring until the autumn. These 'set aside' areas are good for wildlife and save you much regular work, and they can be 'recovered' by cutting low down again a couple of times in late autumn. Such strips and areas can be cut either with the mower raised high or with a trimmer and should not need attention more than a few times each year. By cutting the sides at all, you stop them growing up and falling inwards and give a semblance of tidiness. Although this technique is not to be recommended out front in an uptight suburban setting, it is superb for the rear of a larger garden or in a wild area or orchard.

A green lawnmower could save you a lot of work in an orchard or similar. Providing you fence well, geese are no trouble to look after and they will keep an area of grass neat and tidy for you. They'll fertilise your grass for free and give you huge eggs, plus they are the best burglar and intruder alarm you can find. Geese really are a serious option and are employed instead of sheep to cut the grass around distilleries in Scotland because of their use as alarms. Sheep and other four-legged fiends do not go with gardens but geese will save you a lot of work if you have much grass to maintain. They will not eat nettles, plantains and thistles but they keep the grass so well cut that you only have to deal with the odd patch of these weeds. In fact it is nice to have a few of these weeds anyway as they bring in so many insects when they flower.

MINI-MEADOWS, BULBS AND BUNDS

One of the great advantages of rarely cutting grass, other than the immense saving of work, is that it brings in so many different creatures which you wouldn't get on a neatly cut lawn. Anthills, for example. These are not immediately the most inspiring garden feature but they attract something else. Let the ants carry on undisturbed and if you're lucky, one day a woodpecker will arrive to attack the hill. In the UK one of our most beautiful birds, a red and green woodpecker, actually attacks anthills as often as trees. I'm really chuffed when I see one, or more often hear one, at work in my garden. Glorious.

Above: Bulbs provide the perfect excuse for not cutting the grass.

It was the search for sweet sounds of wildlife that led me to remake my garden quite profoundly. Originally I'd wanted to set up my garden to do three things: firstly to grow as much of my own food organically for the highest quality in variety and flavour; secondly to grow many scented plants for my pleasure; and thirdly to prove to critics that an organic garden could be as productive and neat and trim as any other garden. And I also hoped that I'd be able to do all this in my spare time.

Spare time, some hope. I never had any spare time. I was always mowing paths and trimming edges, weeding day and night and carrying more water than a small canal. I managed to have an immaculate, neat, beautifully tended garden but it damn near killed me. And it was nothing to do with being organic or not, it was entirely to do with a desire for man-imposed order and geometry, and onerous work loads. You can only cut and edge so much every week. What is more, my garden, though organic, seemed a bit empty, almost sterile.

Well, one summer's evening, I'd gone to visit some friends, the sort of people who let their dogs do the gardening, all five of them. As I sat with them in their pleasantly lush garden, I couldn't but help notice the sound of crickets. I remembered there had always been crickets in my childhood gardens, so why were there none in mine now? I went home perplexed. I wandered around my garden and indeed not a chirp, save for one. I followed its direction and it was coming from one of my neighbours' gardens, one whose gardening skills had till then failed to impress me. There at the far reaches of my garden where it abutted his, was my only cricket. And a couple more crickets were sending back chirps from over the hedge. His garden was obviously the source and what was similar about both his and my friend's gardens was the unkempt appearance, the uncut long grass...well, where else would you expect grasshoppers to live after all?

'On continental Europe there are many gardens with meadows instead of lawns.'

I started cutting the centres of the paths short but grading the sides, leaving as much as possible uncut. I left the areas furthest from the house uncut, and in corners, under bushes and trees and in front of hedges I planted bulbs, and cut these areas but rarely. Within two years my whole garden started to chirrup on warm summer evenings. One day I was overjoyed when a visitor asked me: 'What on earth is this?' This was a strange thing, a golden coloured worm, as long as my hand is wide at full stretch and not much thicker than my hair, winding its way up around a tall grass stem. I had no idea but a learned friend identified it from my description as a Mermis, or Thunderworm, a Mermithid nematode; a rare creature only found in old grasslands that is a parasite of grasshoppers. I was thrilled – it means I must have built up a thriving population of grasshoppers. And by saving work into the bargain.

On continental Europe there are many gardens with meadows instead of lawns. These are cut but once or twice a year to stop shrubs and brambles moving in and to keep the fertility low so

that the wildflowers prosper amongst the grasses. Such an area is very low maintenance, good for attracting wildlife, and getting bitchy comments from neighbours worried about their property values. As a large meadow area is difficult to get away with, work piecemeal and justify your laziness. It is necessary to leave the leaves of bulbs exposed to the sun until they wither away (about six weeks or so) after flowering finishes. So if you plant large numbers of bulbs in circles around trees and shrubs standing in grass, along the base of hedges and in swathes across the lawn, then these areas should never be cut until a month and a half after the last flower has bloomed. Perfect excuse. So make sure that along with the snowdrops and crocus there are some poet's or pheasant's eye narcissi, as these are very late flowering – almost in early summer. When you eventually cut the grass in these bulbed areas in mid-summer, the removal of the long overgrown sward will leave a stubble that will not regrow vigorously. You will not need do another cut for a couple more months, unless the summer is unusually wet.

Likewise I now leave grass bunds – long grass with wild flowers and bulbs – under my runs of brambles and other trained fruit. I used to have immaculately cut grass from the path itself to right under the canes. However, I started to allow the grass to grow up and the wild flowers to bloom. I planted bulbs as my excuse and have been well rewarded by the different creatures each strip has encouraged. Sure, they compete a bit with the crop but the contribution to wildlife is fantastic – especially the number of ground beetles and ladybirds that live in the bunds. And I find that now the birds steal less fruit, because they're worried one of my cats may be concealed in the long grass. So I don't need to net as carefully anymore, and more work is saved.

It turns out farmers have been doing a similar thing; leaving a narrow strip of uncultivated soil to grow grasses and wild flowers. Apparently every square foot of long grass in the bund 'grows' a ground beetle. Ground beetles eat the eggs of many farm and garden pests and so are useful friends. If saving work by not mowing a strip of grass can produce more of them, well that's brilliant. More pests destroyed and we don't even have to lift a finger.

Right: Now where should I put that deckchair?

4 effortless weed control

We must weed. If we want to save work then we must weed efficiently and effectively. We have to weed to prevent our favoured plants being crowded out. We can garden without ever mowing or even watering, but you can't simply neglect weed control. Given any opportunity, plants we don't want will crowd out the ones we do. That's nature – our plants are not in the best place compared to the weeds who wish to oust them. Weeds are weeds because they are more vigorous and spread more easily than our garden plants.

Garden plants that spread quickly are weeds too, though you may not realise it soon enough. (One important tip for the novice: avoid the gifts of other gardeners. It is rare for an old hand to give a new gardener a choice plant but they will give you carrier bags, boxes or even barrow loads of the most invasive plants just to get rid of them.)

Regard the following plants with care. They are each useful in the right place but can also become a problem: mint, lemon balm, ajugas, lamiums, euphorbias, false valerian (*Centranthus*), feverfew, Himalayan balsam, honesty, bluebells, forget-me-nots, poppies, violets, sisyrinchium, ornamental grasses, bamboo, any bramble, Russian creepers and, on a bigger scale, any large tree especially conifers and leylandii, laurel and privet hedges.

Weed control is the part of gardening that requires the most ruthlessness and timing. You cannot spare weeds; they soon establish and become harder to kill, and they multiply. The old saying 'a year's seeds is seven year's weeds' bears repeating here. You must get on top of the weeds initially and never let them get away. Once the worst of them, such as bindweed, is loose among your garden plants, you have all but lost the game. But you don't need to kill yourself in the process.

I had a friend who had a fairly average-sized garden with a typical lawn in middle and beds around the outside. She was a methodical person and each weekend she cleared an area of the border of all weeds. The next week she did the next section and so on. By the time she got back to the starting point many weeks had passed and the weeds there had regrown. She never managed to get the whole border clean because she never worked backwards keeping the areas she had cleared clean.

All year she toiled round and round, pulling up weeds and taking them to the compost heap. For a few seasons her plants did well but then they faltered. First of all they were deprived of topsoil, as it was continually taken to the compost heap on the roots of the huge weeds she pulled. Secondly her plants suffered when she pulled the huge weeds because their roots brought with them the intertwined roots of her valued border plants.

Pulling the weeds out from among plants also risks damaging their foliage, that is, if they have much as the weeds probably choked it anyway. A few years of continual weeding had eventually reduced the level of the beds to where you risked falling off the lawn and injuring yourself. So now kneeling on the edge, my friend has to bend double to reach down to her border. Mind you, the sunken beds stay moister which is some small comfort in our dry East Anglian summers (when we get real ones).

WEED CONTROL: 'TRADITIONAL METHODS'

The 'pull them all up' approach might be termed the traditional way of weeding. In mid spring the desire comes on the gardener to do something with all the weeds that have grown up in the borders – when they look out and realise they can't see the garden shed for the nettles. Vast amounts of sweat and toil are expended as the weeds are all pulled up. The garden plants left exposed have no leaf or flower where the weeds were choking them; some even fall over without their support. Still the compost heap has benefited. Unfortunately by early summer the weeds are all back. Another bout results and, if it's dry, the scorched earth policy works for the rest of summer till the first autumn shower puts the weeds back on top again. Garden plants do not give their best with this sort of treatment.

The traditional hard-work approach was for the whole area to be ripped up and dug over, removing every last vestige of weed root and then replanted with the newly divided plant stock. Nice if you could do it, but it is difficult to remove every root from the top layer of soil and you can never get them all, especially the deeper ones. And weeds coming in from the neighbours or neglected areas nearby always return. It is impossible to keep an area weed free if roots from other gardens have access. There is only one effective solution: you must dig a deep trench and line it with plastic before infilling it again. This barrier will

work against most troublesome but shallow-rooted weeds such as ground elder, nettles and so on, but may not work against equisetum or bindweed, which are very deeply rooted. An alternative or an addition is to have a wide grass path running around your perimeter and your beds in the middle. Most weeds with rambling roots will come into your path's soil from the neighbours but as they grow up through the grass they will be cut back with regular mowing and are unlikely to persist and grow far enough to reach your border.

Of course, you can also be philosophical and regard collecting the shoots from invading roots as a way of

Weed-preventing trench

1. A short drop from a border into a bed allows weeds, and turf to soon grow into the border.

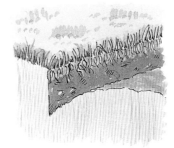

2. A deeper drop stays neater longer.

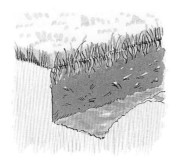

3. A deeper drop with a raked back border is better still.

Above: Plastic rings, easily made from cut-down drinks bottles, keep off the pests, and the hoe too...

transferring fertility from next door's garden to yours. After all, once weeds are collected they are an amazing source of free fertility – especially as so many of them accumulate important trace elements. Indeed, a weed seed in the soil is a package of nutrients the plants can't get at. Until it rots or germinates, the minerals inside are unavailable. As soon as it grows and is hoed under, these minerals change form and can be 'eaten' by our plants. So a flush of weeds need not be problem but a source of fertility provided it is hoed or mulched out of existence peremptorily. Weeds that have become established are difficult to eradicate, though sometimes it's better to have perennial weeds than to replace them with annuals.

WEED KILLERS AND FREE WEEDS

I was doing some landscaping work at a farmhouse set in the middle of fields of cereals and reached by a long lane. This was very rural, the 'road' was two tracks with a green strip up the middle and a similar strip on either side where the car wheels occasionally ran, all between verges of brambles, nettles and so on. The place had been bought up and modernised by a city couple intent on a quick profit, who had tarted it up for sale.

Intending to make it 'neat' they had employed someone to spray all the weeds that were 'ruining' the 'drive'. Well, the spray sure worked, everything was dead and brown on either side and up the middle of the lane. Fools, thought I, as I planted up their garden for them. Next year when I returned the lane was green again, but this time the strips were not the old mix of low-growing perennials but a medley of the weeds that spread by seed. Whereas the old drive may have looked rustic, perennial weeds were controlled by the passage of cars, which pruned them back. Their place had been taken by groundsel, annual meadow grass and dandelions. These weeds seeded ferociously onto the drive itself and then each vehicle pulled the seeds along behind in its slipstream. When the weeds arrived at the farmhouse they invaded all the beds and borders as well as the gravel paths and the rest of the drive.

Nature abhors a vacuum, and bare soil. Any bit of soil will soon be colonised. Weed killers give only respite and though they may have their uses, such as keeping asphalt car parks weed free, they are not much value in many garden situations. It is not sensible to kill off everything in an area and try to keep it

Below: No space for weeds here.
Opposite: Oh the toil, the toil...

Above: Plastic sheet mulches are effective and convenient but ugly and encourage slugs and some diseases.

bare. And where they really might be of use they don't work well, such as on equisetum and Japanese knotweed. As the battle is only ever won temporarily, the best way of keeping out weeds is to have even more vigorous plants choking them out. In full sun the best plant is grass and in shade ivy. These two ground-cover plants will effectively exclude all others and they can be kept neat with a nylon-line trimmer or shears every now and then.

Other vigorous plants, such as mint, can be used to keep out weeds and indeed there is some aggression to be found in many species. Evergreens cause year round shade and the leaves of some even give off chemicals that hinder the germination of seeds, preventing weeds – or any other plants – from starting underneath them. Walk through a pine wood and you'll often find the ground bare, even though the shade is not that intense. The popularity of heather and conifer gardens owes much to their low labour requirements as they suppress weeds fairly effectively themselves. Likewise little grows below a leylandii hedge or a privet. These rob, dry and choke out any competitors very effectively.

One plant in particular, the Mexican marigold (*Tagetes minuta*) is recommended as very good at choking out weeds and gives off secretions that also discourage harmful soil organisms. In the UK this plant needs starting off in pots under cover and then planting out when the weather warms up, at about a foot's length apart each way in a big block. The luxuriant growth chokes out almost every other plant, even couch grass. At the end of the season plants are cut down and composted, and the area dug over or levelled for planting. I have tried this method

and although it worked the nettles nearly won. I reckon the use of a good light-excluding plastic-sheet mulch is more effective.

Certainly in most situations, just covering the weeds with a mulch they cannot get through does the job. For years I used old carpet, upside down, but it's now in short supply and I use layers of cardboard and newspaper instead. Opaque plastic sheet, or even old plastic sacks, is the easiest mulch to get and use. It is very useful for small areas, particularly around a newly planted tree or shrub. It is less good on a slope as water runs off it before it has chance to wet the soil below.

Research has shown that you can significantly improve the growth and performance of a new tree simply by keeping weeds, and other plants, away from it while it is freshly planted. And not just a piddling little circle as big as the mean hole you dug, but a great big area as large as possible. This weed-free zone makes more difference than digging a bigger-than-adequate hole or adding more water or fertiliser than the minimum requirements. Weeds, or any other plants, compete so strongly that the new tree loses out if there are any within close range – and that means as close as the tree's own height. Rather than try to hoe such a large area, put down a temporary plastic sheet mulch for the first year or so but make sure the rain can get through and underneath.

Below: This is the minimum area to mulch and keep weed free around the base of a newly- planted tree.

Mulching between plants with a barrier is such an effective way to deal with weeds that I'll say more on it later. Unfortunately the nicest-looking mulches are the loose ones like shredded bark which are ineffective against some sorts of weeds but very good at stopping others germinating. Most weed seeds, whatever they are, must be close to the soil surface and many need to see the light to germinate. A thick mulch on top of them simply stops them ever getting started.

PERENNIAL AND ANNUAL WEEDS AND TIMING CONTROL

There are just two sorts of weed: those that grow from seed and those coming from the roots of established weeds. The former are fairly easy to deal with as they have few reserves to call on. The latter can be very persistent and difficult to get rid of.

Few weeds germinate and set seed in less than a month or two; even the fastest takes many weeks. Thus if you hoe or weed every week or two, you keep these weeds from seed from multiplying. Even if one is missed during one weeding session, it will probably be got the next.

But weeds coming from bits of root have big reserves; even if you chop them up each bit can make new leaves and roots. Miss one of these and the next time you come back it is bigger and tougher to kill with a mass of roots. If you chop the leaves off and leave the roots they resprout; chop the leaves off again, and they resprout again. It can be demoralising but success is simple and is all to do with your timing. If you remove any plant's leaves persistently enough and frequently enough, the roots expire. But this works only if you can take all the leaves off the roots and do so before the plant has made back the energy it took to make the leaves.

Chop their tops off every week till they never come up again. It does not matter whether you do it by hand, with a knife, with a mower or trimmer or flame gun or hoe. Just remove every leaf every week and sooner or later the roots die and wither away. Try it with a house plant if you don't believe me, and if it's still alive after a year of this treatment I'll give you your money back.

Above: You never need weed or mow a stepping stone.

When I was expanding my gardening round, I was taking on some gardens maintained by one of the good old boys who wanted to be sure I'd look after his customers as well as he had over the years. He came and looked around a few I was already maintaining and then took me to see the new ones. He showed me a garden that belonged to a doctor, and asked me what I'd do when I started the following week. I pointed to a rose bed which I reckoned needed a hoeing as it had some weeds getting away. Then he asked me what would I do the second week. I said I'd hoe it again to finish off the weeds that had recovered. He then reckoned I was a foolish fellow and supposed I'd hoe it yet again the third week.

He explained that it was all well and good to do so, but the doctor would not see the benefit of having a gardener. If I was to hoe the same bed every week the weeds would disappear and never show again. How then was the doctor to appreciate the gardener's toil if it was not seen to make a perceivable difference week on week? The bed had to be allowed to get weedy so it could be seen to be hoed and raked clean. Whatever I could find to do during the intervening weeks, I must never hoe the same bed several weeks in succession. Very few weeds would appear at all and I would have made myself redundant. It was an unwritten rule not to work yourself out of a job, just as the wise rat catcher always puts a healthy young pair back. Thus to make sure I never hoed too often but only every third week or so, I took in hand the long and tediously lucrative hand weeding of the cracks in the brick paths and patio. On alternate weeks I trimmed the hedges and newly installed topiary, which I must say became some of the neatest in the area.

SHARP HOES MAKE WEEDING EASY

I've given talks all over the UK to gardeners both amateur and professional and I almost always pose them the same two questions. The first is 'Do you ever use a hoe?' and the second is 'Have you ever sharpened it?'

It's amazing, in all the audiences over far too many years to recall, that there has only been a smattering of gardeners, (including very few of the allegedly professional), who have ever sharpened their hoes.

Listen! A hoe is a knife on the end of a stick – the idea is to use it to chop weeds in half. No more no less. That's it.

Have you ever tried to slice bread with the back of the knife? A knife needs to be sharp or you can't pull it through string, let alone the fibrous heart of a tough little weed. How can anyone expect hoeing to be easy work if it's done with a blunt knife? Sure, a hoe gets dull as you work, but that's no reason to start with it blunt. I put a good edge on initially with a grinding wheel then every five or ten minutes I touch it up. I carry a carborundum stone in my pocket; they're made for sharpening scythes but they do a grand job on hoes and knives too.

Naturally it also helps to hoe on a windy bright day when the soil is just dry on top. But do it whenever you can – any slicing up will certainly slow weeds down, even if they do not die immediately. The books all talk about hoeing backwards to avoid treading firm the weeds you've just hoed. Personally, I prefer to work forwards, look where I step and save falling over my plants for other occasions. Books also make a fuss about the different sorts of hoe. Basically there are two sorts. Those you push and pull with a blade parallel to both the handle and the surface of the soil are called Dutch hoes and are the quickest to use. The other sort are draw or swan-necked hoes with the blade at near right angles to the shaft and soil. These are slower and harder to use as they are used with a chopping action. They are also useful for drawing soil around the bases of plants but have no advantage otherwise.

With both sorts of hoe, a light thin springy blade is what you want. What you are sold is a great old lump of soft iron, vaguely hoe-shaped and with an edge that would hardly do a child's seaside spade credit. Worse still are travesties in stainless steel

at precious-metal prices. Stainless steel will not take an edge good enough for a hoe and certainly will not keep one for long. A stainless-steel spade may be a good investment if you have a sticky clay soil (a stony soil will wear away stainless steel in no time), but a hoe should be of the hardest springiest steel available. My favourite hoes have pieces of old scythe blade replacing their worn-out ones and this seems the best material for those who can make their own. Otherwise, look for a good old one but put a longer shaft on it as this makes easier work, especially if you are taller than average.

HAND WEEDING

Hand weeding is essential: there is no other way to get at weeds coming up in the middle of clumps of herbaceous plants or among tiny seedlings. Some crops such as onions are better hand weeded than hoed, as any damage to their rather brittle foliage or swelling bulbs is often fatal and they are also shallow rooted. Pulling weeds, as mentioned above, does too much damage to the root systems of nearby plants. Most of us don't

Below: Too delicate to hoe, hand weeding is essential here.

realise how extensive a root system can be – even a humble beetroot may have fine roots extending to many yards in all directions. These are too small for us to notice but are easily damaged if weeds are pulled up by their roots. Far better and less work is to pull the weed with one hand while severing the root with an old sharp knife. I use old kitchen knives of the sort that rust – they keep sharpest. A hand-held hoe is another option but you'll have to look hard to find one as sharp as an old knife. If you are hand weeding then you are probably kneeling; either wear knee protectors or take an old rug or newspaper to make it more comfortable. No work is as hard as uncomfortable work. And do not lift each weed up into a barrow but collect them in a shallow bowl or dustbin lid first and empty it when full. Try to spot your precious plants first and carefully tease away the weeds in a circle around these. Then clear the weeds in the areas between them.

WEED CONTROL ON PATIOS, PATHS AND DRIVES

Nothing spoils the value and appearance of a house as much as a weedy entrance. Concrete and asphalt drives only have problems in the cracks but gravel paths and drives get weeds coming up everywhere if you are not careful. First of all do not make work; do not let weeds seed onto gravel anymore than onto bare soil and do not let leaves build up and rot down either. The leaves provide leaf mould and make gravel into a perfect growth medium, so rake them up and compost them. Gravel is very good at germinating seeds but if it is deep enough they either get disturbed or shrivel before they reach the soil proper. Thin gravel is soon colonised: once you've got rid of the weeds in a gravelled area, apply more gravel and it will stay much cleaner. It is light work to rake thick gravel and done regularly is very effective weed control.

First you have to get rid of the weeds already in the gravel; you can't hoe and on large areas hand weeding is too much work. Light-excluding mulches work but probably a flame gun is the best answer; these run on paraffin/kerosene or gas, and burn with a roaring bright blue flame that sears every leaf it

Above: Boiling water will soon see this weed off.

touches. The aim is to pass this intense flame over the weeds, rapidly damaging their leaves – you can see them go a darker green – but not to burn them away. The damaged leaves then weaken the roots and a second pass a week or so later finishes off most that regrow.

You can hire flame guns and the upmarket ones come with wheels and a hood so you just trundle them along the paths and drive. At the opposite end of the scale, a small hobby blowtorch is the perfect, if slow way, of eradicating weeds in a rockery. Each week every leaf of any weed is seared individually, weakening the plants and eventually their roots expire. With care this can be done without harming the rightful inhabitants. In the same way, a hobby blowtorch will soon deal with all the weeds coming up in cracks in concrete, brick, paving and so on. Obviously, you must be careful and never use a flame gun near inflammable plants such as conifers, or near cars, gas tanks, wood stacks, etc. You should wear all the right

LEAST-EFFORT WAY TO RECOVER A WEED-INFESTED BORDER

This is one of the commonest problems. What to do depends on the severity and form of the weed infestation and the age and value of the border plants. Whatever the situation the weeds have to be stopped from spreading into the area from a neighbour's garden or other beds with either a plastic barrier or a wide belt of regularly cut grass as recommended earlier. Likewise, a border abutting onto a ditch, hedge or wild area full of spreading weeds needs isolating in some way, or replacing.

One of the simplest and easiest ways of reworking the average garden with least effort is to swap the lawn and the borders. If you lift old turf you find very few weeds are in the soil and it can be dug over and made into a new bed very quickly. Thus the lawn can be rolled up and put aside, anytime in autumn, in mild weather in winter or during early spring. The turf will keep for several days rolled up but must be spread out and watered if it's to wait longer before being laid on the new site. The plants from the weed-infested borders can be dug up, split up and planted in the new bed while any surplus can be left in place. Level off the old borders with bought-in topsoil and lay the turf on top. As the weeds, and any plants, come up through the grass, they get killed off by the regular mowing, while naturally the new bed should be dead easy to keep clean.

If the old border is full of shrubby plants too big to move this reworking may be difficult. It may be better to propagate these plants from cuttings in a nursery bed for a year then rework the lawn and borders, planting the new stock and burning the old.

An alternative is to kill off all the weeds between established plants with impermeable mulches. This doesn't work if the ground is also full of bulbs; these must be dug up and moved first. Strips of light-excluding black plastic sheet or woven material are laid down between all the important plants and then covered with a thin layer of a decorative mulch. This forces the weeds underneath to emerge only in amongst the stems of the shrubs, where they are disadvantaged by low light. (Once a week they have to be weeded out by hand.) As they can't get leaves into light, the weed roots under the plastic get exhausted and wither away.

Above: Do not let leaves build up and rot down on a path; gather them up and compost them instead.

protective clothing and have fire extinguishers ready. Because of all this hassle I've looked for alternatives and found that I could effortlessly kill weeds, especially over a smaller area, with a hot air paint stripper I bought in a DIY store. This handy little electric gun is rather like a hairdryer, it cooks leaves quickly and seems safer than a flame gun. More expensive but much safer was a steam wallpaper stripper, and a pressure steam cleaner was even better and quicker. For spot treatments you can even use a steam iron (watch out if your partner catches you using it in the garden). And talking about being in hot water – a kettle of boiling water will kill weeds if slowly poured over them. Whenever I make tea in summer I pour the hot dregs from my kettle over weeds in cracks in my patio paving, getting rid of them one or two at a time.

LEAST-EFFORT WAY TO RECOVER A NEGLECTED GARDEN

If a whole garden is neglected, it is foolish to rush in and change it before you have seen it through a season or two. That insignificant shrub may be a joy in mid-winter and bulbs may appear, at any month, from almost anywhere. Make notes of places that are in dense shade, where water lays, areas that dry out hard in summer or where the snow sits for longer, as these are hard places that need a more careful choice of plant.

Decide what you want to grow, where you want it and plan it all carefully on paper first. Take the time to do a good job – it will be less work. Old fruit trees can often be rejuvenated with a little pruning and a bit of soil improvement. Old hedges can be recovered and even shrubs restored, so do not rush to replace everything at great expense of time and labour.

Most importantly, clear the weeds away first, thoroughly. There is never any point in planting if there are still perennial weeds in the ground. In difficult cases it is often simplest to put the whole garden down to grass, to cut it regularly for a year or two, building up the fertility and eradicating weeds. Then you can plant trees into (generous) circles cut into the turf and likewise beds and borders can be simply cut out of the turf and forked over ready for use. The turf can be used to patch elsewhere or it can be rotted down in a stack under a plastic sheet. It will turn into a fibrous loam perfect for potting or adding back to beds.

GETTING RID OF PERNICIOUS WEED ROOTS

One of the problems I am often asked is what should gardeners do with the roots of pernicious weeds that they have dug or pulled out of their garden. I used to recommend leaving them in the sun on a concrete path or a sheet of plastic until they had withered, when they would be safe to put in the compost. Then I discovered that the Romans had a much simpler method; they just drowned the roots under water. A bucket or barrel will do, pop in the roots, add water and weigh them down. A month or

Above: Weed seeds and roots soon rot if immersed in water. Adding a layer of vegetable oil (such as oil that has been used for frying) will keep down any smell as well as mosquitoes.

so later you have rotted roots ready for the compost heap, plus a liquid to add with them or use as a liquid feed. This method also gets rid of almost all seeds, which rot very quickly under water, so it is a perfect method for pre-treating weeds that have set seed.

FEED WITH WEEDS

Following on from disposing of pernicious weed roots and seedy weeds under water, I wondered what value the liquid produced may have. I was overjoyed to find out that even bindweed has some use: its root extract seems to have some fertility value and I fed my tomatoes in pots with it to advantage. Of course, we have been making comfrey tea and nettle tea for some time but weed-root soup can now be proudly added to the list of liquid feeds. I am, however, careful not to rot down weeds with diseases on them as I suspect this could be a source of problems for crop plants. To make weeding easier, all around my garden are discreetly placed plastic dustbins. These used to hold the weeds until I collected them for the compost heap but now they are pre-digesters, turning them into a liquid feed and a slurry to eventually add to the heap.

Above: Wastes buried in a trench suit marrow or runner bean plants.

EASY WAYS TO MAKE COMPOST

Weeds are the main constituent of most people's compost, together with grass clippings, leaves, prunings, kitchen wastes and the unwanted surplus from the vegetable garden. The usual method is to add these in layers to a bin and when it is full to start another, while the initial lot rots ready for use. Now it may be hard work. but it is less work in the long run if you turn the heap out when it is first full, mix it all up and repack it. This will cause it to heat up and make a better compost. It needs to mature for half a year or so, then be dried out by removing the sides but leaving the top covered. Once the material is dry it can be sieved; the sieved material is like soil and ready to be used for top dressing, potting or mixing in when planting. The spoil that won't pass through the sieve needs the junk removing then the bits can go back to inoculate the next heap.

To make all this less effort, do not put in things that will never compost such as glass, metal, stone and plastic. However, almost anything that has ever lived can be added and will disappear. It is not a good idea to add meat scraps and fats as these do attract vermin. I feed mine to my hens but you could give yours to the birds, or a neighbour with a dog. And if you want to make better compost, chop everything up small and mix

it well, and make it moist. An activator will speed it up, but don't buy one – use nature's own. Urinate onto your compost, or into a can first. Nothing makes compost break down as quick as urine – though chicken manure and nettles are next best.

Gardeners with little space can use a worm composter to eat their waste, but these can cope with very little at a time. It's easier to make a hole in the ground and fill this with the waste, then cover it up with soil. Plants such as a potato or runner bean or marrow will thrive on top of a hole full of rotting garden waste. You can make a trench instead of a hole.

But the best composter for the least work is an old refrigerator or dead deep-freezer unit. Put the materials in one of these and the insulation causes them to really cook. True it does smell and is wet, but you get a liquid feed for free and the temperatures reached produce a compost almost free of weed seeds, saving a lot of weeding later.

Below: Cute if finicky compost container complete with pumpkin plant to recycle the waste.

MAKING A BONFIRE BURN BETTER WITH LESS EFFORT

Some stuff just has to be burnt, be it thorny or diseased. If you have a lot of woody material, maybe you could offer it to someone with a stove who could use it, but more likely you will need a bonfire. Do not pile all the rubbish up in a heap and then spend a day trying to light it. Stack it somewhere off the ground and cover with a plastic sheet till you are ready. This will keep it dry but a stack attracts wildlife, especially hedgehogs. To avoid casualties, make a frame of iron poles off the ground on top of a few bricks or stones. Pile some of the dry stuff carefully on this and light it from underneath with a ball of newspaper. As it burns down add more from your stack. Do not pile it all on at once or add wet or green stuff – it will smoulder and not burn properly, making far too much smoke. By burning up off the ground, material burns quickly and cleanly. The ash can afterwards be added to the garden for its potash content –

gooseberries and cooking apples need it most.

The things you need never burn are leaves. All over the autumn landscape gardeners waste their time, and fertility, polluting the air with smouldering piles of leaves. True, they have to be knocked off low-growing shrubs and evergreens and brushed off the lawns, paths and drive. But burn them? Leaf mould is the finest material for adding to potting composts or enriching any soil and is just rotted down leaves. Leaves lying on grass will kill it but they are easily collected with a rotary mower. Being partially chopped and mixed with grass clippings makes them rot down quicker or stay in place as a mulch. I reckon the laziest way to rot down the leaves is on the beds where they fall and they don't blow around if you pile some more mixed with grass clippings on top of them. Alternatively, you can put them into a compost heap in moderation, but it's easier to cram them into plastic bin bags and hide these out of the way somewhere. By next autumn or so they will have turned into bags of leaf mould ready for use.

Below: Burn a little refuse at a time on top of a grate such as an old gate for most effective burning.

no more digging

Many regular garden tasks have been made hard work by the experts, old boys and traditional garden design and hardware. Especially such antiquated customs as the 'autumn dig'. I do not dispute that a good dig over an area initially is a good idea; it is indeed necessary in most cases. It is not so much to break up the ground – the natural soil layers are probably in far better condition left undisturbed – but to remove roots and rubbish. Digging is done so that existing roots from nearby trees and large shrubs are evicted from the site. Unfortunately roots from nearby trees and shrubs will try to grow back in again so need excluding with a barrier such as a sheet of plastic to line their boundary. All weed roots are removed along with wires, bicycle wheels, bricks and old radio batteries and other junk you seem to have to extricate from almost any piece of ground.

Once the soil has settled, it gives the new plants an unfettered run and hopefully enables them to grow bigger and faster than they would have done without the digging. I would even be happy to recommend you adopt the Roman method of digging to a depth of about six feet: this gave them excellent results though, of course, they had slaves to do it for them. However, reasonable results can be got from most soils with slightly less effort and certainly without the annual ritual self-abuse of the regular autumn dig. It is amazing how most vegetable plots are turned over every year, despite there being a plethora of books and research showing there is little advantage to all the strenuous effort involved.

Now, if you want a bad back go ahead and dig away, but I advise that you would be better employed turning the compost heap or even just going round with a barrow and weeding old ladies' gardens for them. (My favourite method of getting vast amounts of compost material, cuttings, brownie points and almost unlimited cups of tea and cake.)

DIGGING VS NOT DIGGING.

I must confess I am totally prejudiced in the no-dig argument. I am willing to concede that a few of my crops could be improved if I dug over their bed the autumn before, but I can't be bothered. I can get the same increase in yield from one good watering. According to some trials, the increase in any year from digging is much less than the increase from adding more water.

Opposite: If you walk on a plank you need never dig again. Mind you, fixed beds and paths are easier stil.

The increase from digging is in the order of about ten per cent, mostly coming from the increased breakdown of humus into soluble fertility. It's a short-term gain at the expense of long-term soil structure and water-holding capacity. Of course this does not matter so much if you are applying copious quantities of manure or compost. But if these materials are not added, humus depletion can be a serious problem. By contrast, adding water probably encourages humus formation and for almost all normally flowering crops, adding extra water will give a doubling of yields about nine years out of ten in drier areas. In wetter areas, extra watering may not do so much good so often, but in drier periods it offers much better returns for the effort involved than digging. And which is easier? Watering or digging?

If you insist on digging, then at least be methodical. Work up to it, warm up first, and do a little at a time. Use a long-handled spade, stainless-steel in sticky soil, and move only small chunks at a time. Do not incorporate muck in a layer and never ever turn over perennial weeds and imagine they will die away – it's out with their roots if you are digging. Working from a board will stop the soil compacting under your feet. Do not dig when the soil is claggy, wet or frozen. Employing someone else to do it is cheaper than visiting the osteopath.

I have not regularly dug any of my forty beds for nearly two decades now. Although I grant you I'd see a small improvement with potatoes for having the soil dug beforehand, I cannot see the sense in digging for anything else, save possibly salad crops. Trials and reports have shown that, for the vegetable bed, regular digging is least advantageous. In fact of all parts of the garden, there really is least sense in digging the vegetable bed. For an average piece of ground, or a flower bed or herbaceous border there is a gain from digging every seven years or so to break up ants' nests, mole runs and so on. But crop rotation on the vegetable bed creates sufficient soil disturbance anyway. The harvesting of roots like carrots and parsnips, and the trenching, earthing up, and harvesting of potatoes means there is never any real need to dig the vegetable bed. Ironic isn't it.

Below: More water improves yields more than more digging!

Above: These bottle cloches are great protection but the plants would benefit from being more widely spaced.

Of course, the experts can always justify why they have to dig – which is a load of rubbish. For example, digging to incorporate a layer of muck under the plant's roots is now shown to be counter-productive. Few crops like muck underneath them: it breaks the capillary network bringing water and minerals up from deeper layers. Muck can pack down into an anaerobic slab that stops plant roots from penetrating further. In bad cases, it may even poison the crop if the soil is wet, cold and heavy, causing manure to give off ammonia which burns away plant roots.

Another fallacious reason for digging is to incorporate a flush of weeds. This is an admission of poor weed control. If they are little weeds then a hoeing would be easier work; if they are bigger weeds, burying them is laying up a store of trouble for the future. And their fertility will be washed out by the winter rains as they rot there rather than in the compost heap.

However, the perverted logic that amuses me most is the claim that we dig so the frosts can break the clods down into a fine tilth for sowing in the spring. Excellent advice this, but exactly how did you get the clods in the first place that need to be broken down? By digging, of course. That's right, we dig in the autumn so the clods we form can be got rid of by the time the plants come back in spring. Brilliant logic isn't it? And why do we want a fine tilth over the entire vegetable bed?

Naturally we need to make a small area with a fine tilth where we can easily sow leek, lettuce and brassica seedlings to transplant out later. But we don't need a fine tilth to transplant those leek, lettuce or brassica seedlings into. We don't need a fine tilth to plant potato sets or onion sets, or shallots, or garlic, or tomato plants, or courgettes, marrows or pumpkins, or broad beans, French beans, runner beans or peas.... Of course, we need a fine tilth to sow small seeds we must sow in situ such as carrots or parsnips. But how many parsnips do you want? If I only want a dozen or so, why should I sow a thirty foot row? In fact if I wanted a thirty foot row I could expect only about thirty decent parsnips from it, maybe forty if I pushed it. So why sow half a packet, only to thin out nine-tenths of the crop later? You don't need a fine tilth down the whole row: a spot the size of a coin every foot or so will do. You can make such a spot in a second with a kitchen fork, sow three seeds and firm them down and cover them with a wee plastic bottle cloche. Thin them out later when you remove the cloches. Meanwhile the cloches mark the sites so you can hoe between with impunity.

This is much easier than digging all over so the frost can make the tilth along the whole row and for a yard either side. Anyway, if you want a fine tilth just cover the soil with a mulch – particularly a woven fabric one – when you move it aside you will have a lovely tilth.

Below: A nice mulch keeps the fruit and leaves of these tomatoes clean.

The main reason people dig is they have always done so and because in some cases, they have made the ground compacted. If the soil is compacted it may be helped by digging, but it is better not to compact it in the first place. How do you compact soil? By walking on it when it's wet. The usual scheme of having rows which vary in width depending on the crop, guarantees that every bit of soil gets walked on this year or the next. And as the whole gets compacted the whole gets dug.

RAISED BEDS, FIXED BEDS, BLOCKS AND ROWS

In the flower garden we tend to make our beds and borders (if we design them at all) fit the garden space with most emphasis on their shape and possibly some thought to their depth and the direction they will be viewed from. They may be dug over initially but from planting on they are fairly static. In the productive garden we are demanding much more of our plants and clearing them all annually, thus we need to give crops air and light all round if possible and easy access for us. Traditional row-cropping fits the bill but causes compaction. A major improvement is to go over to fixed beds: these can still have rows on them but the paths always remain paths.

Indeed, fixed beds really should be called fixed paths, as this is the salient point; by making the paths permanent they are never dug. The beds are always in the same place and are usually about three or four feet wide (about a metre or a bit more) so all parts of the bed can be reached from the paths. As the bed does not get stood on, it does not need digging. If you still want the exercise, go ahead, but there really is no point.

Fixed beds can be any length you want. I reckon if you make them about fifteen foot long then it is not too long to tempt you to walk over the top rather than right round. Also, if you make the side paths between beds only a foot or so wide, you can't easily get a wheel barrow between them when the plants are

Opposite: A good path saves work.

full grown. If the cross paths at the top and bottom of a set of beds are a bit wider, a barrow can be parked at either end of a bed and it is not too far to carry weeds or produce to it. As with

'we need to give crops air and light all round if possible and easy access for us.'

traditional rows it is a good idea to align beds approximately north-south, so they get sun on one side in the morning and the other in the afternoon. Rows or beds running east-west can be completely shaded by a tall crop on one side.

Many people go on to raised beds. These are fixed beds with altitude. The idea is that raising the beds means less bending for us and it's also good for the plants. The coldest air behaves like water and runs off raised beds into the paths between, keeping the plants marginally warmer. Even more importantly, raising the beds allows the plants roots to stand above waterlogged land – that's why I went on to the system. My vegetable plot is low lying and in wet winters it pools with water; raising the beds by only a foot above the paths drains

Below: A system of raised beds can be convenient and saves the back.

Above: Raised beds warm up sooner, drain sooner and so mulches such as these grass clippings are more useful.

them and keeps them standing like little islands in a grid of canals. I still lose many over-wintering crops to root rots in bad years, but less than I would on the flat.

I also used raised beds when I had a garden with only inches of soil above solid chalk. Scraping soil from the paths and the rest of the garden, I managed to get a decent depth of topsoil to grow in. However, if I'd not been scared of the effort I'd rather have excavated a bed into the chalk and filled it level, than had to pile the soil up on top. Raised beds are not all advantage: true they dry out and warm up more quickly, but then they also get drier and more baked in summer (any god willing), which is not so good if you want to grow spinach but great for tomatoes and sweet corn.

Drying out can be a big problem. Irrigation with a sprinkler wets the paths as well as the beds and wastes much of the water, including any that runs off. Likewise, rain can be wasted. Raised beds are harder to keep moist unless you go for something like seep hose irrigation. A glorious alternative is to pay the extra water bills and enjoy flooding the paths between the beds. By making mud piles at the ends, any path between two beds can be flooded. In this way, the surface of the beds stays dry so weed seeds do not germinate and slugs and snails don't move around, while the water seeps in sideways to the roots. This encourages the roots to grow down instead of forming the mat that sprinkling encourages. Unfortunately, you do use a lot of water unless your path is well-trodden clay but I have never yet achieved yields as high as the times I used this trench irrigation method.

A great drawback to raised beds is that it is sometimes difficult to keep a loose mulch on top, especially if you have lots of birds about. Mind you, my cats have a lot of fun in summer as the network of sunken paths between forty raised beds gives them ample opportunities to chase and ambush one another, as well as scare the birds.

Just face it: fixed beds save a lot of work and make the remaining work easier, whereas raised beds are really a specialised method and are not a work-saving direction to go in. Many people want to cram as many beds as possible into a small space and raise the sides with planks or similar. This is an unnecessary expense and creates places for pests to hide in and rots to start. Raised beds, if you must have them, are better made with sloping sides and ends; not only is there nowhere for pests to hide but this maximises the growing area and maximises the aeration and insolation of the soil. This means more air can penetrate and more sunlight is absorbed. Four sloping sides also give you some different micro-climates: the top is open and windswept, the sunny end brighter and drier, the shady end cooler and moister, while the sides are in between. A uniformly planted crop will experience differing conditions and respond accordingly with variation over the whole bed. This means some will mature early on the sunny end, some later on the cooler end, and the bulk on top somewhere in between, thus spreading the harvest over a longer period. Those low on the sides get cooler moister conditions and their roots can run under the path so they can make the most growth. Or you can use the differences to suit certain crops: say tender plants at the sunny end, salads on the shady end and sheltered sides, and main crops on top.

LEAST LABOUR WITH PATHS AND EDGES

We are mostly concerned with the beds in the productive garden – the paths and edges are less considered than those in more ornamental areas. But they can be a source of trouble if not well planned. Between flower beds grass looks best and it doesn't stick to your feet, but it does need work to look after it. Grass paths are the most economical to install but foolish to have if they are narrow and have lots of edging. Worse, they encourage slugs. Between vegetable beds it's best to use the bare soil and include it in the hoeing regime. You could gain more planting space by putting down stepping stones and growing crops between them.

Stepping stones, or slab paths, are almost maintenance free. They are quickly and simply laid on a bed of sand and can be moved if your plans change. Or you can go for gravel or sand paths; these are prone to weeds but quite aesthetic – sharp sand is an excellent path for between vegetables. These sort of paths will not take heavy traffic though, unless you lay them on

a hard-core foundation. In either case the path material itself needs to be thick enough to rake.

However, I'd counsel against these sorts of paths because of the weeds you have to deal with if the paths are contaminated with the soil or mulch from the beds. If you do have a sand or gravel path, it is sensible to make it stand a little higher than the beds. It is easier to incorporate sand or gravel into the soil with little harm, than it is to get soil neatly cleaned off the path.

Alternatively for more ornamental and soft fruit areas, where mulches of mushroom waste, composted shredded bark and

> ### 'Worst of all are upturned bricks or tiles, which are a haven for pests and weed.'

straw are strongly recommended, using the same or similar material for the paths makes sense aesthetically and will save labour. (Though both path and mulch could be sand, gravel and pebbles etc., these do not ever add any value to the soil.)

One of the advantages of using the same or similar materials for the beds and the paths is that you can dispense with the edging needed to separate the two, though some demarcation may still be necessary. The conventional grass-path edge to the soil in the border is just cut into the turf and needs redoing every few weeks. Ghastly plastic and metal edgings rarely look good or last well. Wooden edging rots too soon and shelters pests. Worst of all are upturned bricks or tiles, which are a haven for pests and weeds and crumble continuously, adding detritus on either side and don't allow a mower to cut over them safely. The great advantage of slabs or stepping stones is that they have no edges to maintain, as long as you lay them well and just slightly proud of the soil but set so the mower can be driven over them if necessary. If weeds do grow over the edges of a sunken stepping stone, lift the slab, add sharp sand to level it up and re-lay it closer to the surface. This is less work than continually cutting weeds away. Where weeds grow between slabs, either hook them out with a sharp knife or

Left: A good hard path should stand proud of its surroundings so that any spillage is from the path to the soil and not the other way round.

Clockwise from far left:
A wee grass path such as this is a
tedious amount of work. Why not
simply replace it with paving like its
neighbouring path?

A hard surface is a good idea,
although it might have been better to
have set the slabs right up to the
grass on the left-hand side as the
stones are sure to spread.

Overhanging plants save maintaining
the edges of a grass path, although
the lax habits of the plants here might
make cutting the grass a bit
awkward.

This is a good low-labour design
which will allow its owner to spend
many lazy hours in that hammock.

Small beds make access for weeding
and other tasks easier.

Above: Paint this fence in winter when the geranium has died down.

'cook' them with any of the methods mentioned earlier. Then fill the cracks with grout, sand or plants such as thyme and chamomile so you do not have to weed again.

LEAST LABOUR WITH HEDGES AND FENCES

As we can make more or less work with path maintenance, so can we with hedges and fences. In the first place it takes about the same amount of admittedly different work to make either boundary. A fence is put up quickly but has a limited life. Any fence usually goes at the posts: if they are wood they rot; if metal they rust; both break soonest at ground level. Soaking the post bases in creosote or oil is much less work than painting the panels and will add years to their durability. I doubt painting a fence ever added a day to its life but if you must, then use plastic sheet or newspaper laid right up to the fence to protect your plants and path from drips. With a palisade fence or similar you can drag a plastic sheet right underneath to keep paint off your plants and soil off your paint. A sheet of cardboard can be used to hold back bits of shrub while you paint behind them.

But forget painting – it's bracing and cross wiring the fence so that it can't move which adds much more to its longevity. Slow rocking eventually breaks the posts or allows panels or poles to drop out. Despite all this a fence is probably the best option for a small garden and at least it does not need cutting every year.

For larger gardens the cheapness and longevity of a hedge, plus the aesthetics and sound proofing all make it more desirable. But hedge trimming can be an horrific task, exacerbated by our desire for a quick hedge and our foolish choice of a fast grower – which of course fails to stop being a fast grower when it reaches the height we want. Just look at the many people boxed in by giant leylandii hedges who only see the sun when it is overhead – if you could look at them, that is. Hedges need only be high enough for wind protection and privacy, but sadly the best hedging plants all want to go to many times higher and so need cutting. Slow growers take longer to reach the required height, but at least there is less to cut off each year. Rather than relying on cutting a hedge, you can plant an informal one, though this will tend to take up much more space. Informal hedges are generally a mixture of plants left to grow fairly naturally and are much like thick shrub borders. Because of their size they are only really suited to the largest gardens. The rest of us need to clip, or pay someone else to.

Below: Laying plastic sheeting over the bed before cutting the hedge will help to protect the flowers and make it easier to collect the clippings.

Above: Laying sheets at the base of the hedge and over nearby flowerbeds makes tidying up much quicker. A flat area between flowerbeds and hedge makes access to the hedge easier, and will avoid damage to the beds.

In either case, if clipping needs to be done, regular trimming is the answer. As with so many jobs, the regularity of the work reduces the total load and/or the bill. Several light trims are easier work than one heavy lopping, and the trimmings are easier to utilise than a skipload of branches. Most mature hedges can be kept neat with but one cut a year if done in summer and if done every year. This knocks the stuffing out of the plant: it loses so much material that it stays pretty much static throughout autumn and winter, with fresh strong growth only resuming in spring. Young hedges benefit from several trims a year to make them bush up, with the harder cuts in winter when they are dormant to encourage strong regrowth. Clipping is easier quicker work if there is no border at the base of the hedge. Grass or a path makes better access for cutting and it is simpler to set up steps to reach the top if they are

required. And do put a sheet down first and cut over it; this saves so much work instead of raking up the bits. Do the sides first from the bottom up, then do the top. Try to pace yourself. As I said earlier, I hate using a mechanical hedge trimmer but they are handy for doing the top of high hedges. This is always the hardest bit and up there you can't see what a poor job they've done compared to shears.

Trimmings from conifers and evergreens are best pushed under them for a natural mulch and wildlife habitat, but not in areas where they may be a fire hazard. Soft green leafy growths can be added to the compost. On a grass path, light trimmings can be collected and shredded simultaneously with the grass by the mower. Heavier trimmings can be bundled together to make havens for wildlife. Incidentally, it is less work to chop up heavy prunings using a hand axe on a log than with secateurs.

6 don't waste time killing house plants

We all love having plants in our house, but a poor display of dying plants impresses few and does not make us feel either comfortable or satisfied. What is worse, we can spend as much time and effort looking after a bad display badly as after a good one well. It is a shame that when we play let's-pretend-to-be room-designers, we do not put as much thought into our choice of plants as we do into the shade of the drapes. And woe betide those who accumulate house plants in the way we collect boxes of memorabilia. 'Oh and this one, I don't know what it is and it's never flowered, but it came from a bit of one at old Uncle Rupert's...' The worst problem is when they do not die quickly and cleanly but hang around filling up the best places. All the sunny window sills are full, and until some recalcitrant plant finally expires, another in a holding bay in the bathroom must languish there until its buds and half the leaves have dropped off.

PLANT CRUELTY

I love plants and, although I wouldn't go so far as to say they feel distress as we do, I'm sure their systems must still feel discomfort or even pain as they wilt or are scorched by heat or cold. After all, they have to respond to minimise and repair damage so some perception is necessary – if only at cellular level. I do not like plant cruelty. Admittedly it is not as heinous as hurting children or other animals; however I feel unease at the sight of a plant struggling to survive against the odds while its dumb owner stares on regardless. The number of times I have been asked 'What's wrong with my Whatdoyoucallit?' only to be confronted with a totally defunct and defoliated stick stuck in a clod in a tatty pot. 'It's dead ma'am!' is the polite reply – from total neglect in some cases, unrealistic expectations in many and just plain lack of thought in others.

I do not wish to be surrounded by dead, dying and decaying bits of expiring life and I'm sure most of you don't either. After all we try to fill our houses, offices and work areas with plants to bring a bit of cheer and naturalness into our artificial cave of dim light and right angles. They are not very cheery if they do badly, and while you may not win promotion on the luxuriance of your desk display, you'll feel better for it. And plants really do make us healthier; they take our waste carbon dioxide and turn it back into life-giving oxygen, they clean the air of dust particles and even remove and break down many airborne gases and toxic chemicals. NASA has found that the humble spider plant (*Chlorophytum*) is exceptionally good at cleaning air and could be used in spacecraft, making it a perfect plant for the hi-tech office, where all sorts of nasties come off the computer systems and printers, to say nothing of the drinks machine.

HELPING POT PLANTS LOOK AFTER THEMSELVES

No work is more wasted than trying to prolong those plants that are at the end of their life. There are different sorts of plants for different purposes. Now, no-one would expect a bunch of cut chrysanthemums or dahlias to last for ever. Likewise, many house plants are intended to be one-shot affairs; they were never meant to be resuscitated for another go. Although it may be possible to grow on and re-flower those enormous hyacinths, that gorgeously scented gardenia or that giant amaryllis, the result will never be as good as the first time – unless you are exceptionally gifted or experienced. Many plants can be persuaded to grow on but it is futile: the same effort would be better employed on more rewarding subjects.

Beware of house plants with massive shows of gorgeous flowers as these are probably short-lived displays brought on with the tricks of the nurserymen's trade, such as artificial lighting periods. Plants with decorative foliage tend to be longer lived, especially those you see in commercially tended displays. After all, if you are renting it out you want something that looks good all the time for the least effort. Unfortunately this tends to reduce the choice to weeping figs *(Ficus benjamina)*, swiss cheese and rubber plants. All of these are robust, almost bomb-proof, but could hardly be said to be exciting. Nonetheless they are good plants for filling big spaces with the minimum of care.

Most cacti and succulents are even more enduring but, having evolved as soft plants full of water in dry places, they have also tended to develop thorns, making them inherently undesirable in the house or office. (Or maybe not depending on your attitude.) However, they are real tough survivors and when they occasionally flower they can be spectacular. Beware the false though; many years ago I was visiting student friends in Paris and wanted to buy them a wee thank-you present before I

left. I wandered down to the famous flower and plant market near Nôtre Dame. There on a misty winter's morning I saw some sweet little cacti with bright cheerful flowers and I thought what a good low-maintenance gift this would be for my friends' top-floor flat, which had a small sunny window sill. They were duly pleased, or feigned so as one does, and I was even more pleased the next time I returned to find my small gift not only

Below: Conservatory plants make a good display outside in summer, and all of these don't need as much watering as just one hanging basket of bedding plants.

still alive but flowering again. On inspection the flowers were dusty – the damn things were stuck on! Mind you, for those with brown thumbs, the combination of fake flowers and a survivor like a cactus is not such a bad idea. I even knew one lady who had plastic tulips that she'd pop into a weedy border just to liven it up and annoy her neighbours, who could not have the real blooms till weeks after hers had stolen the show.

There are some cacti and succulents that do flower regularly and there are even some fairly boring ones that have no thorns. Among these tough survivors, the foliage ones are the most appealing for year-round value. And of course if it's utility and saving work you're after, then maybe your house plants should all be edible herbs. Though unfortunately few herbs love being perpetually indoors, unless on a cool and very sunny window sill. Probably the best choice is the *Aloe vera* as this is an attractive and robust house plant. The succulent stems also ooze a juice that is soothing for burns and skin conditions.

Aspidistras are a traditional house plant: they are among the toughest of all, slow growing and a big clump can take years to form with almost no effort on your part at all. I have even used them in the garden where they unexpectedly survive frosts, so they do not need to be confined to draughty dark hallways once they get too big. Spider plants are among the world's best survivors and produce myriad offspring ready to replace the parent should you lose it. Although the variegated version is most common, there is also a plain green form which I think looks healthier. Similar at first glance is the friendship plant (*Billbergia nutans*), which looks like a spider plant without the sprays of little ones. Once it has been neglected and pot bound long enough, it starts to produce amazing pink, yellow and blue flowers that are truly tropical looking. As this plant is also capable of taking some frost and total neglect, I've also been trying it in the open ground where it survives but not happily. Indoors, though, it is a treasure, and is almost neglect proof. In between in toughness are a host of house plants from the cyclamens – fairly robust – to cape primroses and orchids and other delicate stuff. Well, they're not so much delicate as choosy and are miffy if they do not get their ideal conditions. So don't waste work with the difficult when easy alternatives exist.

Opposite: Spider plants are tough survivors and also clean the air.

Above: Aloe vera makes a useful and tough house plant.

WHERE TO BUY

With few exceptions, house plants are generally tender; this means they are not able to stand frost or severe cold. And they certainly cannot take cold winds, especially if they were raised in a warm sheltered greenhouse. Buying house plants from a market stall is foolish. They may not be too cold in your house but they were half dead before they got there. A cold windy market, or outside a garage or supermarket, is no place for a tender plant. Don't touch them, they're sickening already. And do not believe the market stall-holder who says, 'They're alright love, but I'll give you one off the truck'. I suppose his truck, and the wholesalers', had lovely warm air heating for the plants. Such plants have invariably had a severe check in growing conditions which for plants such as gardenias, azaleas and Christmas cactus causes the flower buds to drop a few days later. Then you can conveniently blame yourself instead of the poor conditions the plants had up till then.

Displays in supermarkets are worse; they are too warm, never watered and the light is too dim, but at least the plants have not been chilled by the wind – only by the transport and storage out back. A large garden centre with a house-plant section is a better place to shop, or even the small florist who grows his own. Buy at these places and take the plants straight home – do not leave them in an unheated or overheated car.

Plants for free can be the best plants, and the worst. You either grow them yourself or get them given to you. In either case, this is an economy measure rather than a save-work scheme. If you want to save money go for free plants, but you'll rarely get anything worth having given to you. Growing your own is next best; it is not a lot of work if you plan it right. Of course if a plant grows quickly and easily it will probably also get too big quickly, but many plants are easy to start from seed and not too demanding. Free seeds come in every fruit we buy to eat. Almost every seed will germinate and there can be few of us who have never grown an avocado or date from seed. And how decorative was it? I bet you still have it, and how does it look now? Was it worth it? I doubt it!

There are some excellent plants to grow from seed, but in return for work done, and the best are bought seeds, not free ones. Schizanthus, the poor man's orchid, is superb and a great show in only a few months from sowing. A custard apple, a lychee or a coconut will rarely make an attractive house plant no matter how long you nurture it. To summarise: if you want a good display of house plants with little work buy good ones (and do not be too mean to throw them out and buy new ones every so often).

POSITIONING PLANTS

This is where so many people go wrong; plants need light, lots of it. Without sufficient they die, though they may take a long time to do so. Our eyes become accustomed to the low light levels in our artificial caves, but even a sunny windowsill in a bright room is still a dark place to most plants. That's why so many of our best houseplants are those whose native habitat is the dark jungle floor or, in the case of ferns, a cave entrance.

If you wish to have plants in dim places, then either give them artificial light, replace them regularly or move them round so each has a spell to recover in a better place before returning. A rotation scheme will save work replacing them in the long run. But choose carefully: plants such as gardenias hate to be moved. Gardenias also like plenty of light but not direct sun, which can scorch them if they're not used to it. Gardenias and many other plants like damp or humid air and are good for the bathroom. It really helps to read the label and check with a good book for each plant's needs.

And do not be so foolish as to put a plant where you can't easily water it. If watering is difficult, it will be neglected and

Left: Positioning house plants in the right place for them will encourage them to give their best, like this magnificent, although short-lived, display of of flowers. Opposite: Cacti are colourful in flower and need little care.

more effort will needed to put matters right. Tender plants should not be kept on window sills that are bright and warm in the day and then frosty cold at night when you shut the curtains in front of them. Either have the plant on a table or position it so that the curtain shuts out the cold of the window at night and not the plant off from the room. Avoid putting most plants in draughty places; plants like a change of air but few suffer draughts. And don't put plants on top of electrical devices – a moment's lack of care when watering can result in hours of wasted effort with insurance claims and installing replacements.

BE RUTHLESS: FEWER ARE BETTER

The commonest problem with house plants is that most of us have too many. Who looks better? The lady with a few fine pieces of jewellery or the one with ten times as many trinkets? Each to their own taste, but I think many would agree that a display of a half dozen well-grown specimens is more impressive than a couple of dozen motley plants filling the same space. It is hard to get rid of house plants as so often they are redolent with memories and have sentimental reasons for their existence. By all means create a memorial window for them, but don't spoil your memories by treating the plants with contempt and negligence. Either give them the proper treatment they deserve so they can serve you well or dispatch them and give the space to the more deserving.

I have a few excellent methods for reducing the number of house plants, other than going away for a very long vacation and seeing what survived afterwards. This the cruellest but most interesting method. When doing the spring cleaning thin out the plant numbers ruthlessly, harden them off and plant them out in the garden. It's surprising how many survive for how long, and some even make good garden displays initially. My Swiss cheese plants made quite an impact and grew enormous during the summer and autumn; they died down in winter but almost made it. I reckon with care these could be over-wintered outdoors, so I'll try again one day. I even put out

Opposite: A few well-positioned conservatory plants are better than cramming them into every available nook and cranny.

several cacti, some that had spines that had done for me once too often on opening a curtain. I planted them out in a sunny dry border and they amused visitors for eight years with no more protection than a sheet of glass in the wettest winters. Unfortunately one spring a plague of slugs did for them, but left the spines in the border for me to find for years.

My favourite but now redundant method had the virtue of charity: I gave the plants to charity shops, jumble sales and bring-and-buy stalls. The drawback is they really only wanted the good ones and there was a danger of bringing back more plants than I had taken. Now that I have achieved some notoriety, I am damned if I can give away a poor specimen so this avenue is closed to me. Nonetheless it is open to the rest of you.

This leaves the standby solution of the unwitting novice; you know, we all do it, as soon as someone young and foolish gets a place of their own, they are considered fair game for dumping all the unwanted household furniture, kitchen appliances and, of course, redundant house plants. It's a marvellous opportunity, don't miss the chance to reduce your collection when it arises.

> 'Who looks better? The lady with a few fine pieces of jewellery or the one with ten times as many trinkets?'

BIGGER POTS AND BASKETS

Although I suggest having fewer house plants, I also suggest you will get more show for less work by giving them bigger pots and containers. Some plants do prefer to be pot-bound to flower well, but given larger pots they simply take longer to get there and it's more impressive when they do. Most house plants do better and take much less work, especially with watering, if they have a generous container. Small pots mean little compost which can hold little water. Also small amounts of potting compost must necessarily hold small amounts of nutrients and so plants will need more care and effort and extra feeding. This can cause more pest attacks. Feeds of liquid fertiliser, unless highly dilute, cause higher sap pressure which encourages scale and aphid infestations. A small pot heats up quickly and cools down quickly while a large container, especially a wooden one, keeps the roots at a much more even temperature.

There is even theft to guard against. If you have several small choice plants by an open window, one is more likely to be 'lifted' than if they are all planted out in one huge lead trough. Stolen plants may save watering but replacements will have to be got. Perhaps a nice show of cacti with plastic flowers might be just up your street.

PROPER COMPOST

Whenever I am at a talk or on a question panel and a poorly house plant arrives, the first thing I do is look at its compost. I'm not so much concerned with whether it is wet or dry but what it consists of. Very few plants growing in pots can flourish in a poor or inappropiate compost. The worst false economy,

almost always resulting in wasted effort, is using anything other than a proper potting compost. Using any sort of poor growing medium will give poor results regardless of all your other efforts and simply waste work. Except for a few very tough house plants, plants in pots must have the best potting compost or they will not thrive. They may die as they cannot use their roots to find minerals further afield or to dive deeper and find water.

Almost the worst compost is garden soil: it is just not open enough in texture or sufficiently rich in nutrients to suit most house plants. A proper loam-based potting compost such as the John Innes series is usually best. Their richness is indicated by the number 1, 2 or 3, the higher being for the stronger-growing greediest plants. Run-of-the-mill houseplants are happy in No 2. (For ericaceous or lime-hating plants use a lime-free peat-, or peat-substitute-based compost instead.) However, I have found neither peat nor other bases are generally as good for house plants as the loam-based ones. Without loam they are too porous, too light and dry out too quickly. And never ever bother to waste

Below: Cyclamens can be put outside for the summer. These might be less work if they were all in one large container.

the effort of bringing home bags of cheap compost unless they're free. Potting composts have to have plant nutrients in them to be of any use; if the bag is old, and worse wet, then much of the value will have gone, leaving the remainder unbalanced. Although it will probably not kill most plants, it will hardly make them thrive and why waste your work potting them up if it does little good? Use old stuff to fill in the bottom of a huge planter or trough. Always buy good-quality new compost from a fast-moving pile of a big-name brand to put your precious plants in. That way you won't waste your effort potting them, only to see them falter and fall.

PLANTING CARE

Feeding plants in pots becomes essential after a time as although a rich compost may have been used it will eventually run out. If space allows, a plant can be lifted out and a thin layer of new rich compost slipped in underneath. Alternatively, a slow-release fertiliser and compost mixture may be added as a thin top dressing but care must be taken not to bury the roots too deeply. A liquid feed is probably the best resort, added very dilute to almost every watering in the spring and summer and hardly ever in autumn and winter. Liquid feeds will burn roots if made too strong so always make them weaker rather than stronger. I use comfrey tea and seaweed solution. I tried fish emulsion which worked wonders but seemed unecological and smelt a bit. Cold tea with no milk or sugar is a handy tipple for most house plants – the spent leaves were always used to blue hydrangeas. If you regularly heavily feed plants that lose a lot of water to evaporation you may build up salts in their compost so at the end of the growing season wash this through with plenty of rain water to leach out any surplus before colder times return. It is wasted work to repot a plant badly, either too deep or too shallow. To repot it and then ram a supporting cane through its roots is also foolish, as is using a pot without drainage holes or one that is manifestly too small. Consider splitting a plant into two rather than slowly choking it to death – a nice pair can look better than one mass. If you are splitting a plant give it a good watering the day before. After removing it from the pot, immerse the root ball in a bucket of warm water and gently shake out the

roots. You will find it is easier to tease them apart this way than when dry. On repotting try to get the roots spread evenly through the new compost. And do not be afraid of firming in the roots; few plants are hurt by ramming the compost into the pot compared to those that suffer from too loose a compost. After re-potting stand the pot in a saucer of water. Make sure the moisture soaks up to wet the surface before draining off thoroughly.

WATER TORTURE

There are two ways to kill plants most effectively and the appearance in either is much the same, often causing one to give rise to the other and finishing off the poor plant. And all through good intention. You see the plant wilt, so you water it and it dies. It happens so often. Letting plants get too dry causes wilting, withering and death, but over-watering also causes wilting, withering and death. Under-watering then over-watering plants – if it does not kill them quickly – selects the toughest and keeps them in a state of misery for years.

It is impossible to give a general rule for watering. Many plants have seasonal requirements, which may be widely different to those of other plants. This is definitely a case for reading the label and checking with a specialist book. In general, you can be fairly sure most plants do not want wet compost: moist yes, wet no. Equally, even when dormant, few want brick-dust dry compost, which becomes difficult to re-wet. (Add a drop of washing-up liquid to warm water to help it get wet quicker.) And all plants will use more water if it is bright and sunny than when it is cold and dark. Most house plants die from drought in summer and water-logged rotting roots in winter.

Houses tend have a very dry atmosphere and house plants can lose a lot of water by evaporation from their pots and compost. Their leaves may appreciate a misting occasionally, which also helps wash off the dust. There are some exceptions: never wet the leaves of African violets, and never splash water on any plants in cold weather. Mist or spray only on bright warm days but never in full scorching sunlight. (And, of course, not if the spray or mist is going to hit or drip onto valuable furniture.)

Most plants are happiest watered from the bottom. One work-saving but effective method is to have them all standing in saucers; fill the saucers with water and go off to do something else for ten minutes. Then refill those that are empty, and after another ten minutes do the same again. Refill any empty ones but empty all the rest. Alternatively stand all the pots in a bowl of warm water for ten minutes and then move them to an empty bowl to drain. Never leave plants standing in water, even as shallow as a saucer, for more than half an hour. (Exceptions include near-bog plants such as lemon grass, and spider and friendship plants, which are very robust, but don't like it permanently.)

Do remember that house plants mostly prefer rain water, and they'd really like it at room temperature. Making watering part of a routine with other jobs means the water can be fetched from the water butt at the same time. Fill up the cans after every watering and leave them, discreetly out of sight, to warm up ready for the next round.

TIES AND BONDAGE

Although most of us spot this problem and avoid it, every so often someone brings an example to one of my talks that has been strangled by its label or tie to the supporting cane (which was also probably rammed right through the roots). Even more frightening are the rare cases of plants re-potted without removing the first pot. This probably harks back to the days of whale-hide pots, but plastics don't rot. And just occasionally I come across an entire edifice of sticks, canes, wires, ties and strings to support some poor plant that would be better served with one or two good canes. If you possess one of these, rip it down now and do a proper job or sell it to a contemporary art gallery.

THE CONSERVATORY AND GREENHOUSE

A sun room usually has a normal opaque roof with large windows catching the full sun, much like an orangery. Its bright window sills are well suited to many house plants, though the atmosphere tends to be as hot and dry as the rest of the house. Many plants would appreciate misting in these conditions. Too many plants in a sun room block the light, so don't make work by trying to squeeze more in.

A conservatory is a rather British compromise. Once it was a greenhouse for conserving plants, now it is half an outdoor room and half part of the house, and not really suited to plants at all, which prefer it more humid than our furniture and fabrics enjoy. A conservatory usually has glass walls and roof but the sides that abut the house are, of course, solid. They are often built as add-ons rather than being an intrinsic part of the house design. There should be one built on every house, doubling up as the roof! This is the ideal place for growing plants as it would be warmed by the carbon-dioxide-enriched rising air, exposed to full light and would be economic if designed to replace the conventional roof on new houses. With fan and ducting such a space could even heat the rest of the house when the sun came

Left: Heavy crops need a good support; cross braces in the pot stop rocking.
Opposite: Everyone's dream perhaps, though given the headroom bananas are surprisingly easy to grow.

out. An inadequately heated conservatory may not be frost free as glass cools so quickly at night. If you want house plants for your conservatory, make sure it never gets too cold. Radiators running from the house system may be sufficient if well planned, but an automatic back up may be sensible or all your efforts could go to waste. Plants in a conservatory get more light from more directions and are much happier than on a windowsill though they still need regular watering and probably misting too.

In a greenhouse proper we are getting away from house plants and into serious hobby gardening. There is no place in the world where so much work can be found to be necessary. Firstly a greenhouse is an ideal place to skulk, either hiding from the weather or a spouse – so there is a natural tendency to lurk inside, making jobs up as you go. Fine, if that's your choice, but don't let it eat up all your gardening time. Secondly, for the unwary a greenhouse is a make-work scheme; the watering, the heating, the ventilating each morning, the closing up in the evening, the range of plants. Especially the range of plants; it's amazing how we expect even more diverse and exotic plants to thrive in a greenhouse than we do as house plants. All sorts of plants from all over the world get stuck on a bench and subjected to the same poor conditions. By all means have a greenhouse as a hobby but don't ask me to save you work if you insist on growing loads of difficult specimens. To avoid working yourself to an early compost heap, you will have to rationalise, simplify and perhaps automate.

AUTOMATIC EVERYTHING

Automatic watering, heating, lighting, ventilation and pest control. These are wonderful ideas until you actually come to put them into practice, when they prove less than ideal, expensive and take more time to install than they save. The problem is this: we grow all sorts of different plants in all sorts of odd places. An automatic system is best suited a greenhouse where all the plants are of the same type and require the same treatment. If you have a big bench of show specimens in pots then it may be very sensible to have them on an automatic

watering system. But it is damn near impossible – well, expensive – to do the same for each windowsill around the house. It can be done, but not for the average situation.

Watering the house plants is hardly a chore until you want to go away; then it becomes a nightmare. You can entrust your pets to anyone, after all their requirements are obvious, but for the keen owner of a wide selection of house plants, it's terrible. How do you entrust all these much-loved plants, which need differing amounts of water, to a friend? One solution, often offered – other than cash incentives – is individual wick waterers

> '**To avoid working yourself to an early compost heap, you will have to rationalise, simplify and perhaps automate.**'

made from raised jars of water with a twisted woollen rope leading down onto the compost. These slowly drip the water from the jar to the plant and can be set up to run for a week or so with practice. I've tried these and reluctantly I reckon a list of individual instructions, numbered and tagged for each plant, together with cash incentives and prizes of duty-free booze will get your house plants better tended than any drip system. And almost the same goes for most so-called automatic systems as sold to amateurs. Of course, if you pay the price you can have anything you want, but a reliable neighbour on a generous arrangement will do a far better job and won't fail in a power cut.

Because I travel so often I've done away with anything other than cacti and succulents that can outlast even an extended winter exploration trip untended. However in my greenhouse and polytunnel I have many plants that cannot be left, and I'm obliged to hire a retired gardener to come and deal with this menagerie. I've tried the drip systems which work wonderfully if they're set up well, but the time taken to do so is immense and they need adjusting again when the plants move round in spring and autumn, when some go indoors and others out. Likewise, seep hoses that you lay on or in the soil either inside or outside save watering time but are most use where a uniform crop is being grown and not for keen amateur's wide mix of plants, each with differing requirements as the seasons change.

Above: Clean windows let in more light than dirty ones, and keeping the number of plants down avoids blocking the light for those further from the light source.

Automatic heaters are a good investment to protect the house, yet alone the house plants, from frost and damp. It is worth having them in a conservatory or sun lounge to back up the house system in cases of very severe cold weather. Fitting small, unobtrusive, electric fan heaters may seem an indulgence at the time but can save a lot of panic later. In a greenhouse proper however, they are an expensive indulgence that will lead to increased bills and more plants being kept. It's a dilemma: heat is so useful but it will never be enough and using it guarantees you'll grow more plants and with much more labour.

For economy, background heat is best provided from the domestic heating system; after that automatic electric systems are the cheapest to install but expensive to run. Automatic gas and oil systems may be cheaper to run but require more maintenance and are relatively expensive to install. Insulating the glass with extra plastic saves bills but cuts down the light, making plants more prone to moulds and root rots. This is a critical factor for plants in winter when low light levels make it even dimmer under cover. Dirty glass cuts down the light even more so it is false economy not to clean the windows.

An automatic lighting system for plants may also make us more cheery if we too are affected by the seasonal dimness. The cost of insulating a greenhouse plus adding artificial sunlight can be offset by the savings in fuel. The plants are happier, warmer and brighter and you just pay a bigger electricity bill for the light and less on the heating. I've tried this and the plants respond well.

Although automatic anything can make sense in the greenhouse, for ordinary house plants it is generally too much work to set up. Except for one essential: automatic ventilation in a conservatory or sun lounge. Very hot temperatures are fatal for most house plants. Having an automatic, but of course entry-proof, ventilator, which opens windows or turns on fans, will make their life much happier.

Plants in an enclosed environment such as a house or a greenhouse are protected from many pests but equally few pest predators may be present. In a greenhouse using biological controls for many pests makes a lot of sense. Even fumigating the pests is possible. To fumigate plants in a greenhouse simply close it up and light a commercially available smouldering device and stay away until all smoke has long cleared. Certain plants are susceptible so check instructions on device. You can hardly do this with house plants in situ. No, but you can take them out and put them into a large box or similar for fumigation with sulphur or tobacco smoke, where permitted. (Certain countries, particularly us Brits, have onerous laws as to what and how pesticides can be used.) Or put the plants on the lawn and give them a powerful hose down before spraying them with soft-soap solution or inverting them in a bucket of it. One or two treatments like this and most pest infestations will be cleared up. Soft soap solution is a safe pesticide; it is a good old-fashioned potash and vegetable-oil-based soap with no additives or detergents (and is sold at highly inflated prices as 'modern' green pest control). The old boys always used to add an ounce or two of Lux flakes to the gallon of warm water to make a grand soapy wash that killed most pests by suffocating them under a frothy film. Cleanliness was next to bug-free-ness. If you keep suffering recurrent pest problems consider ridding yourself of the pest-prone plants and getting something else.

Below: House plants outside can give a magnificent temporary display.

MOVING THEM OUTDOORS FOR A QUICK KILL

As I admitted earlier, I do occasionally dump my uncherished house plants into the garden and plant them out. This is my way of thinning the numbers but, in fact, most house plants like a holiday outdoors for a period in summer – though many do not want to be in full unprotected sun or they burn. Moving them out to decorate the patio can be a good idea. It saves getting patio plants for the summer and usually makes most house plants revive. Many pests and diseases just disappear as the parasites and predators outdoors clean the plants up. However, house plants cannot go straight out in one go. They need to be moved out one fine day and brought in that night, and repeatedly put in and out for several days until they are 'hardened off' and have adjusted to being outdoors in the cold, wind, and brighter light.

All this work can be reduced by initially arranging all the victims together on a table or boxes on the patio and putting them under a light fleece or net curtain by day and a heavier one at night. By introducing them to their new conditions with this protection all the moving around can be reduced to just two moves. But do be careful: move them out too early or put them in windy exposed positions straight away and you may never have to water them again....

And much the same applies at the other end of summer; don't bring plants used to the cool outdoors into a hot dry room and expect them to be happy. When you move them indoors keep them carefully watered as they are likely to need more initially. They will slow down as the lower light levels affect them. Mist the leaves occasionally till the plants get used to the drier air.

SECURITY AND PETS

Plants that get moved outdoors for the summer, such as fuchsias and lemon trees, can be a lot of extra work. They easily blow over unless their pots are heavy and they are well staked. So use terracotta pots, on the large size, with a heavy layer of bricks and gravel in the bottom and plant into a loam- or soil-based compost not a peat or peat-substitute one. Put a heavy stake with a cross bar or two nailed to it into the pot before filling and planting – this will be a more secure support than a cane. Plants are subject to the wind outdoors and more care needs to be taken to make sure their supports and ties are secure and not chafing. Their need for watering increases, indeed I'll come back to that later, but at least they suffer less from pests and diseases outdoors. That is, all except one sort; nice plants in nice pots tend to walk if two-legged rats can see them. A simple security device is to drill an extra hole in the base of the pot and fit this with a bolt and large washers to a chain, fitted in turn to another bolt set in concrete under the pot. For very valuable plants you can fix plastic-covered steel cable within the roots when they are repotted.

Vandalism cannot be prevented except by good security. Thorny spiky plants are a deterrent and they also help keep out visiting pests of the four-legged kind. Two-legged and four-

legged pets can do as much damage as six-legged pests indoors and out. Indoors your house plants may be the only source of greenery, so pet birds, cats and dogs may all savage them. Save work by giving the pets other greenery; most pet stores sell special packs of grass and other herbs just for pets to chew on. Plants can also be protected with a pin cushion of fine sticks preventing the pet getting its head in too close.

Some pets may try to use plant pots as litter trays. I have it on good authority that a mulch of holly leaves stops this problem. My four cats have always been immaculately behaved but they do have their own flaps front and rear. (They like to go out the way the wind isn't blowing, they even change their minds and try the other flap if it's raining hard outside their first choice.) Plastic tree guards may not be pretty but can protect vulnerable stems, and furniture, from becoming feline scratching posts, while foam pipe-insulation sold in hardware stores is excellent for the stems of standard fuchsias and lemons and, in the open garden, for roses.

Below: Valuable plants and pots can walk, but not if they are chained down.

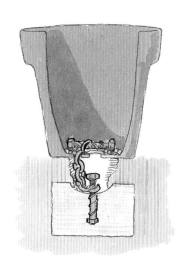

7 saving effort in flower gardens

To keep down work you must always decide on what you want. Many people wisely want no beds of utilitarian vegetables to be tended and just wish to live in a green and pleasant place decorated with flowers. Or maybe they prefer to put their plot down to grass or concrete and their flower garden may be just a small dedicated bed or one area set aside near the patio or in front of a window. For others, their entire garden must be ornamental, or perhaps just the bit facing the road. Whatever the case it can still be a joy or an irksome task to look after.

A well-planned shrub border or a bed of tough herbaceous plants, well mulched, can be a lot of pleasure for little work or maintenance. But add some half-rotting wooden constructions, painted concrete, a gravel path passing through grass with edges of bricks, and even a water feature and you will be kept busy every moment you can spare. A criticism of the instant garden favoured by garden makeovers is that it relies on intruding the physical framework into the picture, to grab your attention and to look different to last week's effort. Little thought is given to the flowers and foliage as seen throughout the seasons, but only to the immediate impact on filming day. All those man-made structures need maintenance as their paint peels, their wood rots, weeds sneak in and the water feature

Above: Good show: a well-planted border leaves no space for weeds and a low-maintenance hard edge between lawn and border cuts down on mowing.

leaks. But plants well chosen will do almost everything for themselves and can be left to it. After a couple of years the instant garden can require immense amounts of labour and materials to return it to a reasonable state. The garden made from plants well chosen and well placed will be looking even better after five years and, apart from the odd bit of pruning or weed control, is not usually falling to pieces!

For a low-labour garden it is more important to consider foliage than flowers for year-round good looks. Dense and well-chosen planting schemes of evergreens can be somewhat boring but have the advantage of leaving no place for weeds and are no work if well mulched. With cunning and planning some more floriferous plants can be included without making

much more work. But once you want to make more than just an ultra low-maintenance garden that looks like the landscaping for an office block, you do need to be prepared for more time to look after it. This need not be arduous and a little knowledge is a great help with the sheer diversity of plants on offer at every garden centre. Such profusion easily scares the novice faced with an unknown amount of work for certain sorts of plant. There are even scare stories about the work needed to maintain various sorts of bed or border such as the herbaceous – though there is some truth to that. However, it is not the type of bed, or choice of plant, but keeping on top of weed control and doing the odd necessary task at the right time that is important.

FOR SHOW, CUTTING OR FUN?

Perhaps you should ask yourself why you are growing your flowers. After all, if the garden is yours to control, you should be able to re-arrange it to suit yourself. For least work and simplicity, put it all down to grass and concrete with a few trees and some magnificent planters, tubs and baskets about the patio and front door. But as soon as you want more out of your garden, you have to make more decisions. Do you want to grow flowers to cut for your home, or to enter a show? Is it to add value to your house and impress the neighbours? Is it to relax after work? Do you just want a few favourite plants around the place, or even a sentimental collection of odds and sods? The tendency is to carry on with whatever beds and plants you inherit, sometimes replacing any losses and usually jamming in a couple of extras each year. I had a customer who was living in her childhood home and cherished the garden and would not let one bed or border be changed. However, the decades had flown by, and the once-opulent garden she remembered could not be the same for her grandchildren. And it was not through want of trying but simply the natural growth of things. True, the hedges could have been kept perfectly as they once were, but not the trees. The once-compact orchard had suffered many losses and the remaining trees had become massive. The bulbs and wild flowers she remembered could no longer survive in the denser shade under those trees – nor under the now huge shrubs in the mixed borders. Here and there a real tough survivor such as a peony or rose would strain from out of a gloomy overgrown bed. Perennial weeds such as ground elder had grown up and, in between the surviving plants, made the best show in the place. The work load to maintain this travesty was no less for the poor show it was, than it would have been to put on a good show. Admittedly there would have been some capital work initially, cutting and clearing, moving and reworking the beds and borders. Even replacing the orchard. But once done the garden would have been what she remembered. Only weeding, mowing and a little pruning took place so the old exhausted plants and borders could never put on a decent show. What wasted work. This is the problem with the unplanned flower garden; it is too easy to spend a lot of time and work to get little effect. All too often it is better to be ruthless and rip the lot out and put in something simpler, more effective – and easier to maintain.

Below: An impressive display of pots is relatively low maintenance and can be made even easier by choosing a single colour theme such as all white.

A QUICK TART UP

You can improve the general appearance of almost any garden without too much work. But remember a proper job takes longer. First pick up all the litter and detritus. Then cut the grass and edges. Weed the paths, drive and patio, then brush them down. Weed the beds and borders by the house properly or, if desperate, cover the weeds with several layers of newspaper and mulch the whole bed with a thick layer of shredded bark. Next go and stand at your main entrance, as if you were looking at it for the first time. Is there anything out of place, any overgrown tree or shrub or eyesore? If these cannot be removed, use some cheap tubs or planters to distract the eye. Fill them with good compost and plant them up with anything bright and cheerful depending on the season. And don't forget the pavement or road outside; a quick weed and litter-picking tidy-up vastly improves visitors' first impressions. In the longer run simplify your beds and borders: eliminate all the poor doers ruthlessly then divide and replant all those plants that have thrived. It may not be tasteful or choice but at least it will be successful.

CHOOSE CAREFULLY, SAVE WORK: DIFFERENT TYPES OF BORDERS

For the keener gardener a quick fix will not do. To make a garden attractive throughout the year is very hard, to do so with minimum labour damn nigh impossible. Nonetheless, nature does much of the work if we but let her – after all, the plants we grow nearly all compete for a living in the wild somewhere. But the situation and the companions will almost certainly not be exactly like the site we can offer in our garden. So it is only to be expected that not all plants will do well. Especially if, like one lady you try and grow a wide range of species. She asked me why she could grow many species of a family in her garden but still kept failing with a few. In nature, species are adapted to different conditions: the lady had put all the different species in one border with the same soil, feeding and watering regime, and micro-climate.

In much the same way, any mixed border can be one of the most attractive or it can be a lot of disappointment or hard work if each and every plant needs a different treatment. Some more

Above: Herbaceous borders need not be hard work.

selective planting schemes, if well planned, can be much less arduous, but though they give a great show at one time they may not make as much of a picture all year round. Some designs are very low labour but give little change throughout the seasons. You pays your money...

The work loads for beds and borders depend not only on their state but the nature of plants in them. The usual mixed border is often an arbitrary combination of herbaceous, annual, bedding, shrub and evergreen beds. To save work overall we have to look at the minimum work requirements for each.

THE HERBACEOUS BORDER

The herbaceous border was very fashionable in past times and acquired a reputation for being hard work to maintain. Which is rubbish, in fact a well-planned herbaceous bed is one of the easiest to look after, simply because the plants are effectively

Above: Eremurus foxtail lilies add height to a herbaceous border.

As to the need for digging up and re-planting the whole bed every three or four years; again true if you want a phenomenal display, and certainly true for naturally short-lived plants such as lupins. But some herbaceous plants such as peony, eremerus and hellebores really resent being moved, while delphiniums need moving only when the clump has become so old and large it has died in the middle.

The greatest advantage of herbaceous borders comes with weed control, especially with those plants such as eremerus, hostas and hemerocallis that die down completely to a few fat buds on a crown. These crowns can be covered with sharp sand and the entire bed can be treated with a flame gun, searing the weeds and any seeds on the surface. A couple of treatments in early spring followed by a heavy mulch and you can have a clean bed all year. Once it is clean of weeds, a heavy mulch topped up every spring will suffice. Alternatively, you can hoe between the crowns of the plants before they break into growth. To facilitate hoeing it pays to cover the crowns with sand after trimming back in autumn to mark their position. This also helps to protect them from slugs. Wide spacing between plants will promote bigger stronger specimens but means more weeding or mulching early each year. Cramming more plants in means they will need less weeding but it will be harder to weed between them.

absent for the winter. Once they have died down it is not very interesting, but it is not hard to maintain. Trimming back the withered stems will maintain some vestige of order. But don't cut the stems back to the ground: leave a foot or so of the stiffer ones standing. These will protect and support the young shoots as they emerge in spring, they trap leaves and loose soil building fertility, encouraging basal rooting, guarding young shoots and buds against frost and mechanical damage, and act as an over-wintering home for ladybirds and other beneficial small creatures. You can compost all the withered stems but as they probably have little fertility value, they are best bundled together and hidden under an evergreen or in a hedge base to act as wildlife habitats.

Other objections to herbaceous borders included the need for staking and tying up lax plants. Today a well-planned bed will have shorter stouter plants buttressing taller ones. Modern varieties have usually been bred to produce shorter stockier plants; choosing these makes more sense and saves more work than growing heritage varieties. More importantly, if you do not apply loads of fertiliser you will not encourage lots of of soft, floppy growth, and probably also suffer fewer pest and disease problems.

> '...a well planned herbaceous bed is one of the easiest to look after, simply because the plants are effectively absent for the winter.'

When making a new herbaceous bed, the most important point is to start with a clean soil with no established weeds. The second and equally important point is not to choose plants that are invasive and spread by seed or rapidly outgrow their allocated space. Known offenders to avoid are thugs of the mint family. (Lemon balm does not spread widely by root as do mints as is often stated, but does seed everywhere.) Lily of the valley, alstroemerias and some asclepias are all dangerous plants as their roots spread widely and sneak everywhere. Yet they are so delightful it's hard to treat them as the weeds they become. Plants that seed everywhere, such as lemon balm and golden feverfew, are always bad choices as dead-heading must be done to avoid incurring even more work. Bulbs, which are so typically herbaceous, should be treated as such and planted in groups by themselves, preferably through uncut grass if native species. Never plant them between other clumps of plants as fillers in a bed as then they make a problem with weeding. If they are spring flowering put them at the back of the border where they will be on view in flower but hidden as they fade and other plants grow up in front of them. If they are summer flowering, give them their own place in the scheme. But do not simply pop them in temporarily vacant gaps as they will encourage weeds by making hoeing difficult. Most spring-flowering bulbs are best planted through grass at the bases of hedges and trees as suggested earlier. If mass planting bulbs, then throw them from a bucket and plant each where it falls for a natural effect.

In a formal bed groups of the same plants, in odd numbers such as five or seven, look better and perform better than singletons. The foliage forms a micro-climate between the plants and the bigger clumps formed look more impressive.

Herbaceous plants, being perennial, have immense reserves and deep roots so the soil they are grown in does not usually need much feeding – except for notoriously hungry species such as delphiniums. But because of the soft sappy growth of herbaceous plants, they need watering to prevent them wilting and collapsing in drought conditions where shrubs wouldn't fare so badly. To avoid doing too much watering too early grow some phlox in the border. These are among the first plants to show droopiness if they get dry and warn you in time to save the others. (Bedded-out daturas also show drought pretty quickly compared to other plants.)

Below: This herbaceous bed will only need a light trim and mulch in winter to make it good for another year.

Opposite: Annuals can give a fantastic show of colour for minimal work.
Above: Nigella is a pretty self-seeder useful for filling gaps.

THE ANNUAL BORDER

The annual border is not often seen, yet it offers colour and variety with very little effort: no soil improvement or feeding at all and not even too much watering. However, it must be done well to save work and look good. An annual border offers great scope for experimentation as you can do it all again, and differently, as you please each year. The skill is not just in the choice of plants and their siting but in getting them off to a good start without a lot of weeds growing up with them. Most annuals do best sown in situ and this means that weeds also get the opportunity to grow and start. You cannot simply sow seed and mulch the whole bed over as the annuals won't be able to germinate. But you can mulch fairly thickly and then carefully draw the mulch aside to sow in the soil underneath. Few weeds will come up in the mulched areas but this still allows the weed seeds in amongst the flower seeds in the exposed strip to germinate, right where they will do most harm. The solution is to cover the exposed strip of soil with a bought-in sterile loam-based sowing compost and to sow into this and then cover the seed with more of the same. (Alternatively sterilise soil by cooking it in the oven or over boiling water: no seeds can survive the temperature of boiling water for long. Commercial loam soil for John Innes is steam-sterilised at 180°F for three quarters of an hour) And do not sow too many – seven plants will make a better display than seventy, or seven hundred, in the same space. Honest, try it. Plants or groups of plants or trees should nearly always be planted in odd-numbered patterns – fives or sevens always look good while even-numbered sets are harder to arrange aesthetically. Make the gaps between the plants in a set small enough so the individuals coalesce to make a full show as they mature.

Most annuals are relatively short so do not require staking or tying. In most but not all species, nipping out the growing tip early results in squatter bushier plants. Good watering initially helps but do not overwater when flowering, and don't wet the petals. Never feed fertiliser, organic or otherwise, to annuals: they will run to loads of soft, problem-prone foliage and produce few flowers. Half starve them and they bloom prolifically, on stunted plants. Water them but don't feed them unless your soil is really poor and you will get bigger plants that bloom well, and give them plenty of space apiece for the best show.

One slight disadvantage to annuals is that most die away after blooming and seed everywhere if their flower heads are not removed. Nigella, pot marigolds and borage, for example are typical self seeders. On the plus side, many hardy annuals can be sown in autumn to make bigger plants the following year and any gaps made up in spring.

With careful sowing, early hand weeding and diligent dead heading, the total amount of work for a good display of annuals

Below: Annual poppies put on a quick show in the most miserable of soils.

all summer is not minimal but a fair reward for your effort. However, the work does have to be repeated every year, and if mulches are used they will need replenishing every time unless you are careful not to disturb them when weeding, sowing or removing plants. It is possible to cut away the dead top growths of annuals and leave the mulch undisturbed, but it is better to vary the sowing positions. The gap opened up should be topped off with fresh mulch and new positions chosen next year.

THE BEDDING ALTERNATIVE

Rather than sow annuals in situ they can be grown under cover, along with half hardy and tender plants, then planted out in late spring as bedding plants to give an almost instant show. This entails either growing these plants yourself or buying them in. The latter is the least work and probably not much more expensive compared to all the costs of growing your own. I suggest you grow your own crops but buy in bedding plants. You can't get organically grown crop plants very easily so better to concentrate on growing crops and leave the flowers to someone else.

Bedding plants give you a good chance to get on top of the weeds by thoroughly clearing the bed before you put the new plants into it. Following a winter planting of pansies or spring bulbs, you may just manage to slip your new plants in between the old without ever leaving space for a weed to poke its head up. Changing bedding displays with the season does give a continuity of colour but you have to multiply the work by as many times as you want to replant, and water the new lot in, and deal with all the weeds the soil disturbance and watering create. Using mulches reduces the work, but these get messed up each time you replant, making expensive replenishment necessary. As the quality of bought-in bedding is dictated by commercial pressure, you rarely need worry about performance, staking or tying. Almost all bedding sold will be low maintenance and give a good show with little care once established. As with annuals, do not feed heavily if at all, as this will just encourage soft sappy growth, fewer flowers and a proneness to pests and disease. In very poor soils incorporate well-rotted manure or compost but not straight fertilisers. Bedding plants benefit immensely from seaweed sprays while establishing but stop once they start flowering.

THE SHRUB BORDER

The shrub border was traditionally massive and rather unsuited to the modern small garden. Too many of the best shrubs got far too big too quickly and so we then had to spend work pruning them back or let them grow, choking out the nicer more compact specimens and eventually hogging the whole show. Modern compact, slower growing varieties worked on dwarfing stocks are often very floriferous but cost much more than nondescript seedlings and mass-propagated common varieties. For example, a cheap unnamed double white or purple specimen of lilac may be good value for its low price, but spend a bit more and get the Korean lilac, (*Syringa palibiniana* or *velutina*), the Persian *S. persica* or the lovely *S. microphyla* as these are all more compact after ten years' growth.

Herbaceous plants stay the same height and just form larger clumps but shrubs get bigger, wider and taller every year. Fortunately, shrubs such as flowering currants, buddleias, winter jasmine or dogwoods can be cut back hard to the ground or near to it, but only if they are so treated every year, as then they form a stool. This is a stump of old wood that throws up strong new shoots, much like the legs of an inverted bar stool, each year to flower and then be cut away in turn. This complete shearing is a simple job and quicker work than the more complicated thinning and training as is often recommended. A trim with the shears is also better with roses as I point out elsewhere in this book.

Below: Shrubs will give a bigger display each year, unless pruned that is.

Above: This restrained border will not take much maintenance to keep it healthy and in shape. Growing fewer varieties of plants would make it even easier.

Planning is everything in a shrub border and rather than rely on pruning to make space, I repeat, concentrate on choosing mostly slow-growing compact shrubs and don't be tempted by any cheap unnamed plants. There are often good and inexpensive choices to be made if you read catalogues from specialist nurseries and purchase mail order. Plant bare-rooted plants if you can get them as then you can be sure they will root into the soil and not stay in a ball. You only plant once, well theoretically, so do a really thorough job eliminating all weeds and improving the soil. And if you are close planting then start pruning everything from early on in their years and do not leave it till they are all lank, leggy and browned out at the bottom. A shrub border can give a fantastic display every year for decades with little work needed once the plants have been initially established but every so often even the most choice and allegedly compact plant may need cutting back so don't put strong growers close to paths. Pruning is really only done because our plants grow out of the space we want them to occupy so extra feeding is very counter-productive and will lead to soft sappy growth and fewer flowers. Of course if it is lush foliage effects you are after then apply more food to the soil but be careful not to overdo it; more well rotted manure or compost is more useful than straight chemical fertilisers as it is less likely to make the plants prone to problems.

Once established, shrubs do keep out a lot of weeds with their summer shade and autumn leaf litter but many perennial weeds will sneak in if not guarded against as this is their natural habitat. And as the ground is exposed all winter when the shrubs are dormant then hardy weeds such as the annual grasses can move in. A good mulch topped up once a year will take care of most of the weed control. Other than that there is little work except for pruning. Although they look lovely, an under planting of spring bulbs can allow a weed problem to develop unnoticed but at least it can be seen and dealt with as the bulb's leaves wither. Do not neglect this weeding or you will have a harder job later.

THE EVERGREEN SHRUB BORDER

Without doubt this is the least labour, unless a perennial weed problem was not properly cleared first. However, once evergreens, including heathers, get going they need almost no weed control. Especially if they are planted cunningly, to meet and form a close undulating canopy. It is hard for most weeds to

Below: Foliage is restful year round and needs little maintenance.

germinate in the dry shade beneath and even if any do, it is likely they will expire before they can reach the light. Moreover, the leaf litter and even some leaf exudations all inhibit weeds too.

There is a certain sameness the year round, which is welcome in winter but less than inspiring in summer, but the lack of chores in a well-planned evergreen bed is exemplary. The permanent ground cover is perfect and being evergreen, is an ever-present source of cover for countless small creatures that then ensure natural pest control and save even more work.

If there are many deciduous trees in your vicinity, remember to brush their leaves off low-growing evergreens or they can

Below: It doesn't have to be planned...

...but planning helps give structure to the planting.

smother them. And it is said you need to brush snow off to prevent the weight breaking the branches. Go ahead, I've got better things to worry about if we get that much snow the plants are in peril.

THE MIXED BORDER

What should be the best of all the borders is more often a case of happenstance, with sporadic plantings of various impulse buys or plants. Now, it's your choice, and it is hard work to rip the whole lot out and start again, but as it gives you an immensely better show and much less work in future, I strongly suggest you take my advice. Many gardeners are reluctant to make the effort despite the future savings and continue to plant almost at random into already occupied beds. What is then created is not a true mixed border in the planned sense but a mixed collection of not-awfully-compatible plants. (In some cases not dissimilar to the planting schemes suggested by many allegedly qualified landscape gardeners.)

There is nothing intrinsically wrong about any plan from the aesthetic point of view. Have what you find pleasing. But wide

mixtures of different sorts of plants soon get reduced to the few most competitive members that choke out their unsuitable companions. This tendency is even worse when planting into a bed or border where existing trees, shrubs or herbaceous plants already have their roots. Then you either have to help your new plants survive or put up with poor results. As the established plants all around soon get their roots into your new plants soil it is pointless enriching or watering their planting sites alone. Enrich the soil in the whole bed or border, dig well and widely where the new plants are going and firm them in well. Then keep the whole bed watered until the new additions have established. Never just water the new plants or you will draw in every root from yards around.

Despite competition and incompatibility between some plants, a mixed border well planned and carefully planted can give the widest interest throughout the year.

MULCHES MAKE LESS WORK

Mulches are the way to save work. By using mulches whole areas hardly need much attention for most of the year, and the plants love growing though a mulch. Well, at least most of them do: it is not a good idea to use thick mulches near low, flat or cushion-forming plants, which can be swamped or choked if the mulch gets onto them.

Once you have got an area clear of established weeds, the easiest and least work to maintain this state is to cover the soil with a sterile mulch. Weed seeds need to be near the surface receiving warmth and oxygen before they germinate; buried under a thick layer of mulch they never get started. Of course, new weed seeds may blow onto a mulch but with diligent care elsewhere in the garden this can be minimised. Any weeds that do start on a mulch are easily pulled, raked or hoed out before they get too big. A sterile mulch is the best as it has no weed seeds of its own. Well-rotted farmyard manure will have many seeds but is still worth applying for all the other benefits.

Mulches keep the soil moist by preventing evaporation – though they can also prevent a succession of light showers ever reaching the soil. By conserving moisture, mulches greatly aid

plants in drier regions. Equally in wetter areas, mulches protect and prevent the soil surface becoming compacted or eroded by heavy rain. A mulch encourages earthworms to turn over and fertilise the whole depth of the soil. The worms don't have to avoid the topmost layer of soil as it doesn't dry out under a mulch. With a mulch above them, the worms are able to work the soil without coming too close to the beaks of birds searching for their dinner. A mulch keeps the soil at a more even temperature. Its insulating effect stops the soil underneath getting too cold in winter and from cooking on the occasional scorching hot summer's day.

Mulches are usually best applied after the winter rains and before the plants have started growing in early spring. The most effective permanent mulches are those with a coarse texture allowing air and water to penetrate but blocking the light from weed seeds. Loose mulches need to be at least a finger's length in depth to be effective, but you can get away with slightly less if you rake the soil level first and then put down several layers of newspaper to form a temporary seal. Initially, this improves weed suppression dramatically and then disappears with time, allowing the mulch to incorporate slowly from the bottom up, as it should. As organic mulches degrade they add fertility directly and add to the soil's organic matter content, improving water retention and fertility. Non-organic mulches such as sand or gravel may mix with the soil eventually but have little effect on its fertility; nonetheless they are excellent for suppressing weeds, look perfect under some plants and they also discourage slugs and snails from moving around.

Coarse mulches such as chunky bark also provide a lot of niches for small creatures; I have been amazed by the number of beetles, spiders and newts I find in my borders where I use such mulches. Unfortunately, the birds also spot this and start to scatter the mulch about, removing some of the wildlife and messing up the appearance.

Sometimes birds and cats messing up the mulch expose the soil in places – or, worse – contaminate an area of the mulch with soil. The simple answer is to have newspaper, cardboard or woven fabric mulches underneath the loose mulch. Mulches do

Opposite: Bark mulches are amongst the most widely used.

Above: Mulches are an attractive way of keeping weeds from starting.

need topping up each year because they slowly break down. It also helps to bury the old surface with its accumulation of leaf litter. Newspaper, cardboard or old carpet are all useful but unsightly but great work savers if used with a more decorative mulch. Likewise woven or pierced plastic sheets; these suppress weeds and let air and water through. However, they are expensive and need topping off with something more attractive.

Utilitarian areas can benefit from plastic sheet mulches. They save so much weeding and are indispensable for recovering large areas without any effort. They should not be left down indefinitely, especially when not covered with a topping, as they degrade in sunlight and it's hard work picking up shredded plastic.

WHICH MULCHES TO USE

Cocoa shell is a coarse brown material that, once wet, forms a very effective weed-suppressing mulch, even in quite thin layers. Which is fortunate as it is expensive, However it is also very good at discouraging slugs and snails. It must be used with care: if spread thickly and wetted down over say, hostas, it may even stop them emerging. One of the best.

Mushroom waste is brown initially but goes light on exposure. It is too fine and doesn't allow air and water through sufficiently if used thickly but is superb from most other points of view, especially price when ordered in bulk. Because of its treatment, it may be unsuitably alkaline for acid-loving plants, and it can lead to unsightly crops of mushrooms. What a shame. I eat them but dare you?

Composted shredded bark is excellent for all ornamental areas. The finer grades are best for areas that need reworking regularly such as annual or bedding beds; the coarser grades make a better mulch for more permanent areas such as under shrubs. Ideally, use a layer of the fine with a coarse layer on top. Bark also makes one of the best and lowest maintenance paths if no weeds are allowed to seed on to it. Constant traffic means it stays pretty clean and the odd weed seedling is disrupted by the constant passage of feet.

Straw is excellent for utilitarian areas such as under strawberries, rhubarb and soft fruit. It makes good paths in the vegetable bed and I even mulch my potatoes with it. It is generally considered unsightly for the flower garden, which is a shame as it is excellent, one of the best and cheapest mulches if you go straight to a farmer for it in bulk.

Shredded newspaper is cheap and easily available. It looks bad initially and soon packs down to make a cardboard-like layer. It's good under another loose mulch but a bit much on it's own.

Sand should ideally be sharp sand, which is grittier than smooth or builder's sand. It makes a very good mulch for ornamental areas but carries indoors on shoes. It is heavy, making it hard work to put on in thick layers, but it is also cheap when delivered in bulk. Sand is perfect for protecting the crowns of dormant plants from feet, frost and pests. Rake up any worm casts carefully on a dry day and add to potting composts. Left in place they encourage weeds to start.

Gravel is also decorative, cheap, and heavy. It doesn't carry on the shoes quite as easily as sand but should still be used with care near entrances to the house. Next to grass it should always be lower than the lawn or it will spill onto the sward, causing problems with mowing. Gravel seems the perfect medium for germinating seeds, but if it's thick enough their roots fail to reach the soil and can be easily raked out. A thick gravel mulch, or path or drive, is very little work if regularly raked, but leave it and it becomes a task.

Grass clippings are most labour-saving mulch of all. Added in thin layers, grass clippings just disappear. After a grass-clipping mulch has disappeared over winter, the ground is littered with countless worm casts and the soil texture looks friable. Put on in thicker layers it forms a loose soggy mulch in the wet and a sort of cardboard when it dries in the sun. In very thick layers grass clippings just make an anaerobic, slimy mess which is of little use and smells quite offensive.

I first started using them in my orchard, putting them in a wide ring under the trees to suppress grass and other weeds. It worked amazingly well, even against annoying weeds such as docks, thistles and isolated clumps of bindweed. The weeds soon push through the thin layer of clippings from the first cut of the year, but the second time they get a whole load dumped on them, and then again and again until they are long gone.

I was so impressed with the benefit to the soil under the trees I started robbing the orchard and every other grassed area so I could use the clippings under my soft fruit and among the vegetables. I even designed my garden so that the clippings could be available as a mulch close to every bit of grass that needed cutting. I made wide grass paths to provide copious clippings to feed the soft fruit alongside and did the same for the borders. I then found them so useful in the vegetable bed and for making hot beds that I have never had enough since. I now accept clippings from my neighbours and I suggest you do likewise, but ascertain they use no chemicals first. And be careful if they, or you, have a dog: their droppings carry disease. Contaminated grass clippings should be used in purely ornamental areas, say under shrubs, and not near food crops.

Leaves make a very good winter mulch for many dormant plants. They protect the roots of evergreens, and add tremendously to both the soil humus and its fertility. They do blow around but once in place they can be topped off with a heavier layer of grass clippings. Grass clippings and shredded leaves collected together by a mower stay put on their own but can heat up if applied too thickly. Most leaves on their own can be piled a foot thick on borders and they'll all be gone by next spring. Evergreen leaves are best under the trees and shrubs they came from, but a few will rot if mixed with other material. All deciduous leaves rot away to leave a fine leaf mould, even walnut leaves, which are said to poison the soil but don't seem to. However it is foolish to put holly leaves on any border you

Above: A mass of summer bedding leaves no hiding place for weeds.

ever intend to hand weed. (Even more so to plant a holly in such a border.) Big leaves such as rhubarb can be used as individual mulch mats to 'spot weed', rather than put them on the compost heap. This is far easier and more frequently done in tropical countries with large leaves such as banana and Colocasia.

AUTOMATIC WEED CONTROL; GROUND COVER

Even though mulches save a lot of work they will still be invaded by weeds if not regularly checked. The price of freedom from weeds is eternal vigilance. But an even better way to keep weeds out with even less work is to get some other plant to grow there.

I had a customer who loved her garden. She would never let me improve it but, like many, insisted I simply maintain it as it was, with the exception of 'encouraging' the new plants she would add. It would have helped if she had told me where she put them, but she'd go out to the garden centre and buy half a dozen new plants, which she'd then sneak in, in apparently haphazard and random spots, with no actual chance of success. Borders at the base of hedges thoroughly infested with ground elder and nettles were treated to a selection of alleged ground-cover plants (including crazily enough some creeping thymes). Most of these could never survive the competition of such weeds and if I hadn't rescued them, would have been dead in no time. Other stronger plants were left to battle against the weeds but eventually succumbed to the intense drought and shade of the hedge. There is no way that any supposed ground-cover plant can get established and choke out existing weeds if it is not itself something far too vigorous for a garden. Ground cover is a battle of plants and the most aggressive wins. Very few can oust weeds without being weeds themselves. This lady's tour de force was planting a border beside a path with ground cover roses. It was a dire choice; the border was only a foot or so wide at the base of a dry wall where the unsuitability of roses as ground cover was amplified by their being pushed back onto the path. Talk about the wrong plant in the wrong place.

In shade ivies are superb ground cover and can be kept pristine by strimming, removing any weeds that emerge. If you are really good at justification then stinging nettles seem to be the best at getting rid of everything else. They do make loads of material for the compost heap but I guess they're not everyone's choice. Most of the prettier ground-cover plants are fine once well established but few are so good as to not need some weeding every now and then. Ladies mantle (*Alchemilla mollis*) is one of the best and suppresses most weeds effectively while looking good most of the year. Some of the hardy geraniums are similarly tough and good smotherers. Few ornamental plants are better survivors as ground cover than lemon balm; the variegated form is more attractive and is almost as vigorous as the green. Under roses ground-cover plants will keep down weeds and to keep the roses' roots cool but should not detract from the roses; violets do very well as does catmint, which allows fairly thick mulches to be used in addition as it will come up through them.

AUTOMATIC PEST CONTROL.

The flower garden has great advantages over the productive garden in pest control. Ornamental plants are usually under less stress: the plants are being grown for flowers, which is what they want to produce anyway, so they are not being subjected to excessive demands. Vegetables are being asked to perform unnaturally well and so become prone to more problems. Many ornamental plants are natural species or little changed from the wild, so they are inherently less miffy from overbreeding. Most flowering plants are grown in a great mixture so the problems of monocrops are removed; pests and diseases cannot build up to vast numbers on an unlimited number of food plants. As plants in the flower garden are mostly all different, pests and diseases that do occur have nowhere to go after their initial success. And the diversity of plants supports a wide range of natural predators to help control any pests that do occur.

With the exception of a few enthusiasts growing nothing but dahlias or roses, there are fewer endemic problems in the flower garden. Slugs, snails, aphids and the rest pose their usual challenges but these often do little harm if you just ignore them. Indeed, I find that most problems sort themselves out; aphids all over a plant one week are replaced by ladybirds the next. I do try to help by providing more resources for the predators so there are always plenty about ready to deal with pests. Basically, the more different plants you have that flower over a long season the more different insects you will support and the fewer pests there will be that get out of control. Some good companion plants are useful, such as French marigolds or *Limnanthes douglassii*. With these plants in the garden pests are more adequately controlled with no effort, but more on companion planting later.

Below: You may have to put up with a few of these if you want song birds in your garden.

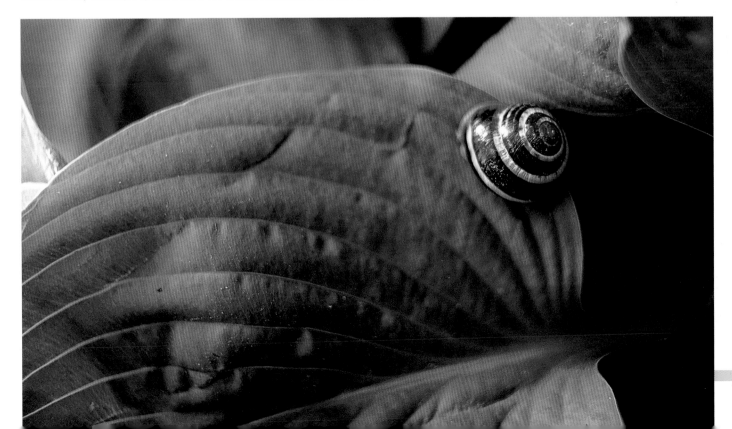

8 don't kill your plants with kindness

We all tend to want to do something to help our plants – often we do too much and sometimes it wasn't needed anyway. I had a friend staying who wished to be of some use in the garden. Being French there was a slight communication gaffe and when I suggested she hoe the asparagus bed she dug it. Now maybe that's what they do where she came from, but with my plants this was a tragedy. I came back later to find her finishing her butchery. She was hot and sweaty and tired, glowing with achievement for having uprooted the soil with its mesh of roots. I took one look at the disaster, smiled, congratulated her on her stamina and suggested a long cool drink. After all, the damage had been done and it was too late to put it right. But all that wasted effort.

Another gardener I knew was always making up special draughts and potions for one plant or another. I guess it may make some difference, but it was all a bit unscientific. I wondered why he spent so much time and effort on his powders and 'fast foods' when a good watering would have done as much good with a lot less effort. Excessive fertiliser use causes far more problems than it ever solves. I went to visit a new customer one day who had rung up with an emergency: their garden was dying and a friend had recommended they come to me for advice. I rushed over, they were right: the garden was dying. The drive was lined

with laurels bearing long yellow shoots and these were the healthiest plants in the garden. The leylandii hedge was brown, the borders looked as if they had been hit by weed killer, but there was not a mark on the grass anywhere. Initially, I was baffled. It looked as if someone with a grudge had sprayed everything with growth hormone, but there was no spray damage on the plants. Then I spotted the clue: granules piled around the stems under some of the evergreen plants. Closer inspection revealed that every plant had had a generous cup full of granular fertiliser tipped around it. The rain had washed in the majority but here and there the evidence remained. A previous owner, a farmer, had left several bags of chemical fertiliser behind. Rather than waste this resource, it was applied in massive doses by the gardener's assistant who, being neither sensible nor horticulturally trained, thought a big feed was better than a small meal.

Plants do need food but most soil is rich enough anyway. Giving them too much is pure poison. The same happens when too much fertiliser is used on a lawn; it just browns out.

Fertiliser granules are lumps of salts. They must absorb enough water to make a dilute solution that the plant's roots can drink without being burnt. To get that water the granules suck it from all round them, even extracting it from living cells by the power of osmosis. This kills most of the microscopic creatures in the soil, which are replaced by creatures that can use the fertiliser as a raw material. And so healthy soil full of nitrogen-fixing bacteria that made fertility for free from the air becomes populated by organisms that break down fertility instead. This is how farmers become dependent on bagged fertiliser to maintain their crops.

In the flower garden we can avoid all this foolishness and wasted effort. So don't make work and push your plants into unhealthy lush growth. Abstain from using chemical fertilisers and only apply organic ones sparingly. Few ornamental plants really need feeding at all; light and water are more important to them. Don't make work and push your plants into unhealthy lush growth. Abstain from using chemical fertilisers and only apply organic ones sparingly.

Below: Water is the most important factor for plant growth.

WATERING MADE EASY

Lugging water around is heavy work and more work can be made or saved with a little thought here than in most areas of gardening. Watering is one of the most enjoyable jobs if all you have to do is to point a hose, but if you have to carry the water in cans it is arduous. One solution is to have water 'on tap' where it is needed most. Long hoses do a spot of unplanned dead heading, deflowering and uprooting as they're dragged around the garden. Putting in a fixed system either underground or hidden away, with quick connection points here and there, allows a short hose to be plugged in and used then taken to the next spot with less collateral damage.

Plants generally prefer their water a little warmer and less chlorinated than tap water especially those in a greenhouse or on a patio. For these plants, it makes sense to fill a barrel, allow the water to warm up and then use it. If the barrel is refilled after emptying, it will have come up to ambient temperature by the next day. If you can't fill a barrel from the tap, maybe it can be filled by syphon.

To make a syphon system, all you need to do is to connect two butts with a hose full of water that reaches to the bottom of both. The water will then automatically reach the same level in both containers, so their overflow levels need to be adjusted to be the same height. Do this by standing the lower of the two butts on a stand, or setting the higher into the ground. Start the

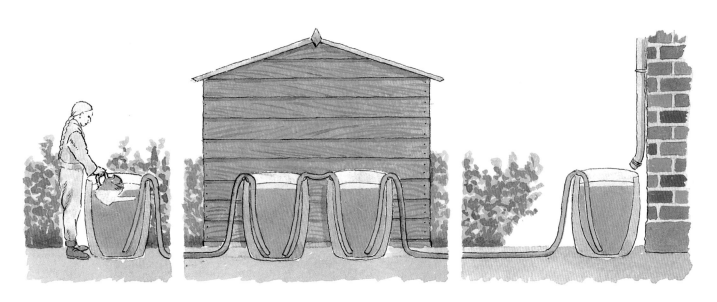

Above: Syphons move water for you and can increase your storage capacity.
Below: Syphons keep the water level, so if you have sloping ground, adjust the height of the butts.

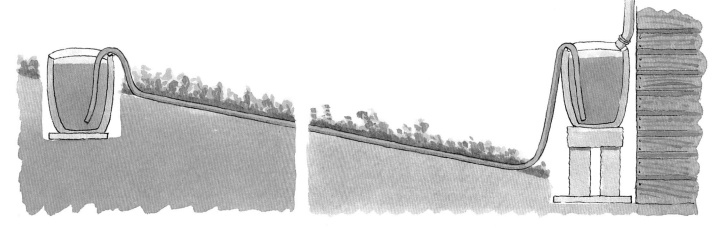

Above: Syphons can be used to connect many butts to increase storage capacity.

greenhouse with a syphon. All I do is dip a jug in and water with ease. When all the water is used up, I leave it and in half an hour the syphon has refilled the butt from the main tank.

And syphons don't just carry water a short distance. Another pipe carries water to a plastic dustbin in a fruit cage at the other end of my garden; it's a long walk, yet the water is always magically there. Syphons can move water from one place to another or even just between adjacent butts. This facility allows several butts to be placed out of sight somewhere convenient and to be topped up by a syphon from a small butt that collects water from a large roof. A small butt that could never hold much on its own is often easier to site where a larger butt would be inconvenient. Water can be drawn from any butt in the system and all will be called upon equally.

Of course, it also matters how you apply the water. To make any difference large amounts are needed. It is of little use just wetting the surface of the soil: this frustrates the plants, causes

Below: Butts can be discreetly placed and screened by plants.

syphons by filling them with water from a hose while both ends are under water – sucking is for kids. If syphons stand for weeks unused, they may sometimes fill with a bubble of air and gas released from the stagnant water. This usually clears itself but occasionally the syphon may need to be restarted. A syphon tube may also kink where it passes over the edge of the butt, causing it to block. A pad inserted here will improve its performance. But otherwise once a syphon system is set up, water is stored and moved about the garden with no effort. And as it is now easier to water it should get done more assiduously.

I have a large tank collecting all the water from my greenhouse roof and from a shed. It is just outside the greenhouse and is connected to a small water butt inside the a mat of surface roots to grow and most of the water just evaporates away, cooling the soil at the same time, which is rarely of benefit. Although some plants may benefit from the occasional syringing down to clear off the dust, in general, plants do better with dry foliage. Wetting the foliage makes it easier for many diseases to start, especially if the foliage is brushed or knocked about at the same time. Sprinkling plants, especially those in flower, is not really a good idea. Far better to apply the water to the roots directly. It is less work to water important plants if each is equipped with its own reservoir: a funnel set into the ground made out of a flower pot or cut-up plastic bottle. Thus each site can be given a great dollop of water quickly that is left to trickle into the ground at its own pace. Alternatively planting in bowl-shaped depressions in the ground enables speedy and successful watering with minimum effort.

I've found trench irrigation to be very effective for improving my plants; they just love it where the water comes in from the side in quantity, thoroughly soaking the soil. It also displaces stale air, replacing it with fresh air as it soaks down and away. This air is pumped out the next time the trench is flooded and so on. On the down side, water consumption is huge resulting in large water bills if you're on a meter. But in terms of plant growth, crop yields and low labour, nothing compares to the effect of adding more water.

In the UK the rain mostly comes in the winter, meaning that there is a water shortage in the soil during much of the growing season. Just adding water allows the plants to perform to their

best – little other work can give as good a result by comparison. Obviously, if your budget can run to it then automatic irrigation is well worth it in labour-saving terms but go for the sorts using drip or seep hoses rather than sprinklers. And in the interests of the planet, it's a bit of a waste to water the lawn just to make it need cutting more often. Watering flowers is marginal, as is established fruit, but do not skimp on watering new sowings, transplants and vegetables – these all need it most.

Left: Watering a trench is a low-work way with vegetables. Water soaks into the beds sideways, closer to the roots, and the surface of the bed stays dry.
Above: A plastic bottle funnel takes water direct to the roots of a young plant.
Opposite: Watering cans are best used in pairs otherwise you're unbalanced.

Above: Sowing in situ usually means either gaps in planting or overcrowding.

SOWING IN SITU VS TRANSPLANTING

Although plants sown in situ are usually the best, success is also hazardous as they are exposed to the vicissitudes of the weather and pest attack while they are most vulnerable. Their lot can be improved by using cloches, plastic bottles and bird scarers, but they are still less likely to give an even stand of plants than the same area bedded out with ready-grown plants a month or so later.

Growing under cover or in a seedbed and transplanting is extra work but worth it for a uniform result or where the plants need a longer growing season than they can get outdoors. All the problems referred to with house plants appear again but worse, when we start to raise dozens if not hundreds of plants to transplant later. The need for sterile weed-free compost good enough for them to grow in, regular potting up, watering, opening and closing the ventilation and frost protection for tender plants does make raising your own a great deal of work.

As stated earlier with bedding plants, you have the choice of paying or doing it yourself. I prefer the latter but can't then complain of the work.

Although I couldn't buy in many of the crop varieties I want as plants, and I'd never get them all organically grown, for flowering plants, especially just to fill up one or two containers, it seems sensible to buy in the few I need, freeing up time for elsewhere.

Whether you buy in or grow your own, plant them out as soon as the weather allows and while the plants are still small. Small plants (not stunted, simply younger) take better and get away sooner than bigger plants. Do not buy 'bargain' giant plants. And don't be fooled by buying plants in flower – a cheap trick worked on us every year by garden centres. You may have noticed how plant centres usually feature plants in flower so that we can choose ones we really like. But when it is flowering is not usually a good time to be planting any plant, especially not annuals and half-hardy annuals such as French marigolds. Retailers know we love to buy things in flower so most plants, bedding especially, are given a regime of artificial light, heat and fertilisers just to bring them to flower. This ignores the fact that the plants would transplant much more successfully, grow away sooner and form better plants if they were not in flower. Buyer beware!

As it is hard to find bought-in bedding plants not covered in flower buds, it is usually worth the effort of nipping them all off before you put the plants out. This gives them a chance to root before having to put on a display as well.

You may also wish to grow perennial or herbaceous plants from seed; this is not difficult and is probably cheaper than buying in the plants if you want several. But if you only want one then buy it – it will be less work, quicker and cheaper.

For plants grown from cuttings, growing your own is very economical and need not be hard work if you are methodical. Take the cuttings in good conditions from healthy strong plants – one good plant bought-in will often yield a half dozen cuttings or so. Remove their lower leaves and push them into the soil a hand's breadth apart in a bit of the vegetable bed or similar spot, and forget about them till next year, apart from weeding. Autumn is the best time for taking cuttings from most shrubs but evergreens and the more tender hardy plants such as lavender are normally rooted in spring.

PLANTING AND TRANSPLANTING

I was visiting a friend one weekend who announced he was pleased to have me 'advise' him on his tree planting, as he had decided to make a screen of trees between himself and a neighbour. I was only too happy to watch – actual work comes expensive but watching's OK. Anyway, I didn't comment on his choice of tree, nor on his buying large ones in large pots (I'd far rather buy smaller, bare-rooted ones than trees with the first twenty feet of each root wound in a circle), nor even on his siting. But by the end, I couldn't help laughing. To dig a few holes, trim and plant the trees and tie them to stakes should

> **'Somewhere in their dim past they had seen some perfidious advertising suggesting the best way to keep roots happy was to incorporate the last dregs of a peat bog in with them.'**

have been a matter of under an hour. He spent more than an hour just looking for his tools! He must have walked a couple of miles between his sheds – it would have been less work to have gone and bought new tools from a nearby garden centre. When the tired old tools eventually and sporadically appeared, then new ones looked even more appealing.

Still, he dug the holes and, under my prompting, put the spoil on a sheet of plastic so it would be easier to clean up the lawn later. Then he suddenly disappeared and returned with a squeaky barrow carrying a bale of peat, which he then disgorged into the holes. I begged him to stop but he reckoned it would help the roots. Eventually I persuaded him not to use so much and to mix it in well with the soil.

I had to explain that when I was first gardening, I got a reputation as being gifted as I could make plants grow where others could not. The others being the local competition, who was not so much a gardener as a patio layer and plant hitman whose idea of tree planting had been as equally misguided as my friend's. Somewhere in their dim past they had seen some perfidious advertising suggesting the best way to keep roots happy was to incorporate the last dregs of a peat bog in with them. Well my competitor didn't just add a bit or make a mulch of it, no, he put a whole bale in every hole. He stood the tree up in it and tucked it in snugly with more peat, drove a stake firmly through the tree's roots and tied it up with his name tag. (Funny how the name of the vendor remains on the labels long after the plant's name has washed off...) The tree would survive a while but, insulated from the soil by a powdery layer of inert peat, the roots stayed in a ball and the water never made it to them. Within a year or two, I'd come along, remove the dead tree and

Below: A sturdily staked tree, but it would do better with a looser tie and a larger weed-free area around its base.

stake, mix the peat in with the soil thoroughly, lime it and put in a bare-rooted tree, reusing the stake, but not driving it through the roots. And, of course, the tree would romp away.

My friend listened but insisted the peat was essential, as was the bone meal he was heaving in. Actually it has been proved that the most important part about establishing a tree is keeping the weeds down around it for the first few years. Improving the soil in a small hole makes little difference. In fact it can be counter-productive; by bathing the roots with fertiliser the immediate area is too enticing. If the roots find all the nutrients they could want nearby, why should they go further afield? Extra fertility is better applied over the whole area and not just near the roots.

When it comes to planting shrubs and smaller plants, the same applies: it is better to feed the whole area and not to set them into enriched holes. (I say the opposite for vegetables but more of that later.) Whether planting trees, shrubs or smaller plants, put a stake in first, if needed. Then tease the roots out when the plant is in the hole. Make sure the tree or plant is set no deeper than it had been at the nursery: you can always tell by the marks on the trunk or stems. If in doubt, plant shallower – deep planting is not conducive to flowering. Firm the soil down thoroughly and tie the tree or plant to the stake and then put a mulch down straight away.

At the other end of the scale, if you have a lot of small plants to put out then it saves work to be methodical, mark it all out, make all the holes, water all the holes and let it drain away, put the plants in and firm them as you go. Do not leave plants lying with their roots exposed to the sun and wind and then go back to firm them in: do it all in one move so they do not get stressed. And do have all your tools ready before you start.

Below: There's many a good crop to be had from an old tree.

PRUNING MADE EASY

Pruning is another make-work scheme: the more you prune, the more you need to prune. Pruning is necessary because the plants weren't given enough space and/or because they were overfed. Plants do not get pruned in nature, browsed perhaps by a cow or windblown but they need no annual trim as such. Hollow-stemmed ones can even die if cut back in winter as the water lodging inside does untold damage. Pruning anything invariably removes some flower buds that would have bloomed, and leaves scars open to infection. Prunus such as ornamental flowering cherries should never be pruned in winter for exactly the last reason; if they must be touched then it's best done in summer. Likewise, all soft fruit is generally better pruned in summer or autumn than winter but given space should hardly need either. Grapevines are the exception – their idea of space is measured in acres.

Ideally then plants shouldn't need pruning, But if they do, it is best done in summer. This takes away a lot of flower bud but also weakens the plant and less regrowth occurs. If you prune in winter, regrowth usually soon replaces everything you removed and you are at the start of a long battle of growth and removal.

I had a customer who had over-fed and over-pruned his orchard, converting the trees to virtual pollards with each branch lushly festooned with a myriad of crowded shoots known as water sprouts (a thicket of vertical spindly shoots emerging from old branches; they are rarely of any use as they are far too congested to fruit). He employed me to restore the orchard to fruitfulness. First I limed the ground, which was old meadow and very sour from the over-feeding of lawn fertiliser. During the winter I removed the obviously dead and diseased wood, congested stumps and large limbs that had to go. In winter you can see the overall structure and what you are doing: it's the best time for removing and shaping of the larger limbs, but it does encourage strong regrowth. There was no need for re-growth on these trees, they had far too much. What they needed was a more open form that let more air and light in, to make fruiting buds not growth ones. The next summer in several bouts a fortnight or so apart, I removed all the whippy water sprouts that were choking the branches, and then thinned out a few of the most congested shoots and spurs. (Spurs are stubby,

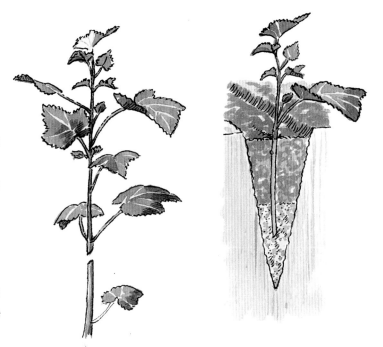

Above: Hardwood cuttings can be made from autumn prunings of many plants. Cut through a leaf joint or just below, remove the lower leaves cleanly and plant in a slit trench with sharp sand in the bottom.

many jointed and branched, and on most woody plants carry mainly flower buds rather than vegetative growth buds; an excess of spurs means plenty of flowers but insufficient new wood being formed to support the huge crops being set, with the final result of a lot of small fruits inadequately ripened.) Taking the material off in summer checked the regrowth. After a second set of summer treatments the following year, the trees were in better shape and the fruit was of a much improved size and quality. Thinking he could now continue, the customer dismissed my services and took over again himself. Back came the feeding, back came the winter 'tidy up' prune and before long he was back to lush foliage and few fruits.

Some pruning is a good idea on most soft fruit, grapes and anything that has a trained form. It is light work but much of it can be avoided by choosing fruit in bush forms and giving them enough space to grow into, as I'll deal with later. In the flower garden it seems only sensible to select forms that will fit the space and not require hacking back every so often. At least herbaceous plants only spread sideways – they don't get taller each year. The bulk of the shrubs in the garden are best kept tidy by cutting them lightly back immediately the flowers have

Above: Roses need ground cover to keep their roots cool and hide their lower limbs.

finished, using shears. This can lead to some ghastly lollipop-like topiary if you don't retain some of the original shape. It is said to be bad to cut through large leaves such as laurel, which are supposed to need pruning with secateurs rather than shears, but I can't be bothered.

If you must prune with a saw, employ someone skilled to do it. It is immensely less work to saw the branch up while it is still attached to the tree. The usual folly is to cut the whole branch off and then to cut it up. Green wood cuts quicker and easier than old, so if you intend it for firewood, cut it up small while it's fresh. Then move it to a heap where it can dry for a year before use.

Young green twiggy stuff will compost: put them in while fresh or they dry and become tough. Mix them with something moist, too, such as grass clippings. Similarly, if you are shredding, do it while the material is fresh. Personally I hate the noise and use the bigger wood as fuel and make wildlife piles from the rest.

Some plants such as dogwoods are cut back at the end of winter, as it is their young stems that are the attractive part. Other plants such as daphnes should never be pruned at all. In fact, pruning an unknown plant can be a mistake so I suggest you get a good book on pruning and read that instead of doing any. The plants will wait another year, I'm sure.

ROSES, AND HOW NOT TO ABUSE THEM

No plant more typifies the counter-productive gardening that expert advice has engendered than the rose. This flower so beloved and typical of England is now less planted than ever – indeed we no longer even want them in our gardens. I postulate this is because rose experts have made them too much hard work for too little return. And where do you see the roses that make you go oooh? Not in the regimented rose beds of the experts but in a neglected and overgrown old garden, where the roses have been left to do their own thing. Of course, like all plants you can coax different performances out of them. If you want bigger flowers you can have them, but roses just left to themselves produce an abundance of blooms. Indeed their only problem is that if anything they are too willing and too vigorous, so once again we must prune to constrain them. Especially if you follow the experts' advice and feed them heavily, and spray them, and prune them harder still.

For the last hundred years or so we have been told how to grow roses by a self-appointed clique of rose experts, who usually also happen to be the growers and purveyors of rose bushes, and who often take turns to be the judges at shows. Between them they have carefully developed a credo that bigger is better (and a hidden agenda that blue petals are desirable). There is nothing wrong with wishing to pursue any area of horticulture, but just because a few aficionados once decided a bigger rose was a better rose then, regardless of whether or not we want bigger roses, that is all we have been encouraged to grow.

Do we want a handful of blooms to win prizes, or do we want a succession of smaller blooms over a longer period? And do we crave the blue rose they keep promising us? After a century of breeding they have still failed to produce a blue rose. Oh, what a shame... Perhaps they could now get start trying to give us disease-resistant or aphid-resistant roses, that have no thorns, need no dead heading or pruning, need no feeding, smell magnificent and flower non-stop from early spring till winter comes again. Or any combination of those desirables. I warrant there is no-one who is not a grower or shower who pines for a blue rose, whereas I bet there are plenty of gardeners who wish they had a better show from their roses.

ROUGH TREATMENT WORKS WONDERS

Many years ago in a previous garden I had a bed backing onto a village hall and the overflow from the toilets' water cistern continually dripped onto my side. I put a compost heap under it but the committee objected, saying it made the wall wet. So I stuck in some roses to hide the wall. With the rich soil and constant moisture these did superbly, that is, they grew a lot

but I never saw many flowers. I did all the proper pruning, burned pyres of thorny limbs and watched them grow but seldom bloom. Then one year instead of doing a proper pruning job, I was in a hurry and I just ran the hedge trimmer through the whole row at waist height and picked the bits up. The next year I was astounded by masses of flowers, produced in several flushes. That autumn I just ran the hedge trimmer over the row again a couple of inches higher. The next year even more flowers, and so on. People started to ask me what I was feeding them on. I'd reply it was a trade secret but I could take on maintaining their roses if they wished...

Look, it's simple: the experts reduce their bushes to a short stump with only a few buds left on it. A few buds make a few shoots which can only have few blooms, which therefore get huge, especially if you feed heavily. Which is also what the experts do; they have to as they have damn near removed all the plant, so it needs the soil enriching if it is to recover. But when you apply a lot of fertiliser to a soil the plants in it get higher sap pressure and appeal more to aphids. (Aphids do not suck sap; they puncture the cell walls and let the sap push through them, extracting the minerals and proteins but leaving the sugars which is why the honeydew that aphids secrete is sticky and turns black with mould.) And because the cell walls are all turgid and pumped up under pressure, it is easier for fungi and bacteria to break in to get at the goodies inside. But that doesn't matter as the experts will be spraying with insecticides and fungicides anyway. And no matter that the plants aren't long lived with this regime, after all they'll soon sell you another.

HOW MY PRUNING METHOD WORKS

What I discovered was that if I left a lot of shoots on the roses, I left a lot of buds and these all broke to make more shoots and more blooms. And as some of the buds were high and some low, some on old wood and some on new, then they all grew at slightly different rates and the flowers came in several flushes. And because the buds were all higher off the ground than when the plants were hard pruned, then there was less black spot on them. This fungal disease affects the leaves, which fall to the ground and leave spores there to re-infect the plant next year. When roses are hard pruned, the first and most tender growths are close to the ground and it is easy for the spores to be splashed up onto them. (Hence the value of a thick mulch of horse manure once the leaves have fallen.) If the plants are pruned less hard then more of the young growths occur higher up, where they are less likely to be splashed with spores. As less wood is removed, less regrowth is prompted and less fertiliser is needed – new growth is harder and fewer sprays are needed. Indeed, it all works for you. Hard pruning causes tremendously strong regrowth, strong vertical shoots with the flowers on top. These can wave about and make a 'cup' in the soil at their base, which may fill with water in heavy ground and rot the stem. So the controversy arose over whether to prune early to avoid wind rock or to risk this and prune late in spring to avoid frost damage to the earlier shoots engendered by an early prune.

Of course, if you don't hard prune and reduce the poor plant to but three buds, then you will not get just three strong shoots taller than you. If you leave a bushy plant with thirty or three hundred buds, you will get a lot of short shoots and a lot of flowers but you are unlikely to produce three tall spiky poles and a prize at the local show. And even after the job is done, the advantages of light pruning pay; you do not have lots of thick heavy regrowth to remove next time, but a lot of short spindly stuff that can be cut with shears or the hedge trimmer instead of the saw and lopper. And as the spindly stems under the flowers also have fewer thorns than strong regrowths, then the trimmings can be more safely handled and disposed of.

Well, for years I have advocated this hedge trimming method of dealing with roses, much to the annoyance of the 'old school'. Then the Royal National Rose Society at its trial gardens at St Albans did a test of a bed of roses conventionally pruned versus a bed of the same roses hedge trimmed, The experts ridiculed the attempt, the old mantra 'pests and diseases' was recited over and over again but, would you believe it, there were more flowers on the hedge-trimmed plants. Sure, the 'proper' bed had bigger flowers, but a lot less of them. The pests and diseases were no worse, if not less, on the trimmed plants, and they kept on producing more flowers for longer year after year. It was not that the experts were wrong, their advice was just inappropriate.

There is not much wrong with following their instructions for pruning if this is done in a restorative manner when the bushes have become too big and dead in the middle. And there is nothing to stop you doing a neater job pruning with secateurs than with the hedge trimmer but until then, if you want to save work, just give the bushes a trim all over, and not too severely.

Below: A rose balustrade as described right.

Above: Tucking in strong shoots, carefully.

Climbing roses have always been treated more leniently. With their stems, the experts' advice would be to trim away the old and tie in the new strong shoots. I agree with the latter part, but have given up trimming out the old. I just wind the new shoots into the old to form a selfholding loosely woven 'basket'. Of course, every so often old and decaying stems need removing to make space again as the plant becomes too overgrown, but in the meantime, the accumulation of old stems makes a paradise for birds looking for secluded nest sites and the saving of labour is immense.

Having seen how winding in the new strong stems worked so well on rambling and climbing roses, I started trying it on bush and shrub roses, instead of the light trim I was then using. Although I was only lightly trimming the rose bushes, they would throw the odd strong stem and I was cutting this back to the general canopy shape. So I tried bending it over, tying it down in a semi-circle, to keep it within the general shape. This did make a little more work but the extra flowers produced seemed worthwhile. Some varieties had stems too brittle to bend so abruptly and these still needed pruning – well, sort of self snapping did it initially. Then I took an idea from the fruit cage and fixed a strong wire in front of and just level with a row of very varied rose bushes. These were bent down and round the wire in either direction and allowing the stronger roses to overlap the weaker but making sure the weaker were on top. The task of turning them into a balustrade was much easier than winding each down onto itself. Now as new shoots are formed they are wound onto this core which gets bigger until in six years or so, it needs to be started afresh. So for those years little pruning as such is done, but just the tucking in of the new shoots as they get long enough.

9 pick more fruit for less work

There is possibly no area in gardening where you can either save as much work or make as much work as growing fruit. It is possible with determination and will power to turn a pleasant little hobby of growing some fresh tasty food into a complex and arcane world of pruning, training and torturing on the grand scale. There is something pleasing about some of the trained forms of fruit trees though the more these are distorted from the natural form, the more work they become. Originally, much of the manipulation was done to get finer fruits or to have them out of season, but much was for aesthetic purposes. The choice is yours: you can have some fruit for almost no effort or you can have bigger and better crops and an immense work load. Modestly improving the quantity and quality requires only a little carefully applied work and, with care, this need not become excessive.

THE NO-WORK APPLE TREE

If you don't have one in your garden now, maybe you knew one as a kid. You know, the old gnarled apple tree that has never seen muck nor pruning for longer than anyone remembers, yet every year produces bucketfuls of gorgeous sweet apples. That is the beauty of fruit, it just appears by magic and all you have

to do is pick it. It is worth doing a little here and there to get better quality, more reliable harvests, but essentially fruits are going to be produced anyway. The plants are doing just what they want; we are not asking them to be Olympic performers like some of the vegetables or to produce massive but abortive sterile flower displays. Plants inherently want to reproduce and usually do this by seed. The fruits are just the sweet sugary bit they package around the seeds to entice us to spread their seeds about for them. That is the deal; the plants give us nice sweet flesh to eat and hope that we will either drop the seeds as we go, or as with tomatoes, the seeds pass through us to emerge embedded in fertiliser ready for germination.

Now, here is one very important point to note about fruits; we are usually after the fruit's flesh and not the seed. (Though with nuts it is the other way round. The almond is almost exactly the same as the peach, except we eat, and have improved, the seed of the former and the flesh of the latter.) From the plant's point of view it is the seeds that are important; not only from its desire to reproduce but also because they take a great deal of minerals, fats and proteins to make, whereas the fruit's flesh is mostly sugar and water, which are easily available most years. Thus the number of seeds made each year determines how exhausted the plant is; the weight of crop merely indicates whether it was a good or bad year. If you remove nearly half the apples from a tree before they have started to swell, the final weight of crop will be nearly the same as that of an identical tree left unthinned.

THINK THIN

If two trees produce crops of the same weight, but one has twice as many apples, then these must be much smaller than those of the thinned tree. And this is what we find with almost all fruiting plants. If we remove many of the fruits when they are small, the remainder swell to compensate. Thinning must be done before the seeds form or the tree is still exhausted by their production. The earlier a crop is thinned, the better.

Thinning is valuable work as in fact it also saves work. As the crop is, say, halved in number but not weight, then the picking itself is also halved, and it is quicker and easier to process

fewer choice fruits than a box full of smaller misfits. When you thin, do so intelligently and remove crowded and congested fruits and those with holes, diseases or blemishes. Thus thinning is also a superbly easy way of controlling fruit pests and diseases. I thin my apples on the dwarf trained trees three times, pulling or nipping the small fruitlets off with my fingers. Once early, once when the apples swell and again when the earliest are nearly ripe. This enables me to remove almost all the poor ones, leaving only the finest to swell to a good size. (The rejects are immediately composted so pests and diseases within and on them cannot multiply; it is a good idea to gather up all those on the ground as well.)

TAKING A YEAR OFF

Maybe you remember an old apple tree that used occasionally to give a wonderful harvest but some years would have no fruit at all. Now this may have been due to a frost or pollination

Below: Thinning these apples would have made them huge.

problem, but most likely it was because the tree was exhibiting what is called biennial bearing. In other words, the tree becomes so drained by yielding a huge crop that it has to take the next year off to recuperate. Some varieties are notorious for this such as D'Arcy Spice and Ellison's Orange. The solution is simply to relieve the tree of excess fruit in an 'on' year so that it does not get exhausted and then it will crop the following year as well.

Unfortunately, although thinning is about as light a job as you can find, it is not easy on anything other than dwarf or trained forms of tree. You simply cannot do a sensible job on a full-size orchard specimen. Plum trees can break their branches with an excessive crop and the solution has to be brutal to be effective – chop off the lowest half of the heaviest bunches with garden shears. But generally a little thinning is a pleasant job to do on a summer's evening and makes tremendous improvements to the final result. With so little actual effort, it must be considered the number one job for most fruit trees.

To point out the value of thinning, I must tell you the story of a co-operative in a peach-growing area. The problem was everyone was trying to compete by growing more peaches, size and quality were low, as was the price, but the co-operative couldn't get the members to improve the quality until someone hit on a simple idea. Each farmer would not thin his own crop but those of his neighbour, avoiding the temptation to leave more fruits when thinning your own.... The result, apart from initial arguments, was that each farmer thinned his neighbours' trees much more ruthlessly than the owner would, which barely reduced the actual weight of crop but the size and quality soared. From then on their fruits were all top grade and the co-operative got top prices instead of selling the peaches in bulk for processing.

STRAWBERRIES OR RADISHES?

Whether you are getting the crop almost for free or having to do some work, its value still depends on if you actually want it in the first place. There seems little point in growing elderberries when as many as you could wish for are on every bit of waste

Left: These gorgeous peaches would have been even bigger if they had been thinned earlier.

ground. Blackberries are the same, the wild ones taste better than most of the cultivated ones, which are thorny brutes that take over most gardens. I almost regret the space and time I've given to mine, except when I remember their value to the wildlife. And, likewise, although I have made a hobby of growing unusual edible fruits, most of them are not very tasty and simply not a good return for any effort, except to assuage curiosity. It is said that the fruit of the strawberry tree (*Arbutus unedo*) translates as 'The tree fruit of which one eats only one'. So unless you are curious don't go to the effort of getting one.

Be sceptical of the puffs of advertisements in the popular press claiming wonderful yields, flavours or prodigious sizes for some unlikely or unheard of offering. If these rare and precious gifts of nature are so good, why are they not on sale in the supermarkets? Usually because although edible they are not tasty! Have you tried the strawberry blite? This allegedly strawberry-berried annual, *Chenopodium capitatum*, is miserable, yet every few years for the last couple of centuries (I joke not), this is trotted out again and again and sold as a new wonder fruit to another crop of gullible novices. They are the most pathetic dry little berries you could imagine – even my chickens can't be bothered eating them. Though they will eat the leaves, ironically, because the plant is a relative of the weed fat hen. Similarly I've seen it claimed that *Passiflora caerula*, the blue passion flower, is hardy enough to grow outside in the UK and produces attractive orange fruits with an edible pulp. True, but first of all it is not tasty and in no way resembles the delicious passion fruit of the supermarket (*P. edulis*), but worse the amount of flesh is minuscule, a mere smear per fruit. The variety *P. racemosa* is marginally sweeter and could be improved to make a great fruit – but leave that to someone else.

CONCENTRATE ON WHAT YOU REALLY WANT

I must admit I suffer the same quandary; which to choose and which to ignore. There is only time and space for some of the many different fruits. And I want to try them all. But to seriously save work you must grow only what you really want. Whenever I give a talk to gardeners I like to ask a few questions: The first is

Above: Do you like these? Then why grow radishes?

'How many here sowed radishes last year, or indeed in any year?' Once I get a show of hands I then ask: 'And how many of you actually ate radishes on more than a couple of occasions?'. It's amazing; although there are always a fair number of radish growers there are rarely many radish eaters. Then I ask: 'How many here like strawberries?' and I am usually buffeted by the wave of air rebounding off the sea of arms. Finally I ask: 'And how many of you grow strawberries?, which is followed by a show of about as few as ate radishes! The Chinese long ago spotted this behaviour and have a saying which translates as 'If you wish to eat strawberries do not sow radishes'.

FRUIT VS VEGETABLES

I used to do a lot of design advice and consultancies for people setting up their gardens to be organic and productive. As with any garden design, it is sensible to set out a list of objectives and to juggle these. At the head of the list so often was the desire to be 'self sufficient' in fruit and vegetables. Poor misguided fools: yes,

it is possible, but to be self sufficient is about as much work as you can ever create, or a very boring diet. The sheer diversity of foods and flavourings can almost all be grown – but is the amount of work worth the effort? Home-made piccalilli is fantastic, but the time and effort growing all the different ingredients and then processing them is phenomenal. I should know, I do it! I think it is worth it for the supreme quality, but the work is substantial.

Many of these advice sessions were for young couples with children and they wanted to have a big vegetable plot so that the kids could eat clean fresh food. Very laudable, but there are several problems with this. The first, and the concern of this book, is the sheer amount of labour needed to set up and run a good vegetable bed, the second is the sense of trying to grow vegetables at ground level in the presence of kids. And the third is the likelihood of ever getting any of that green stuff down the kid's throats anyway.

A classic error from the point of view of saving work is to rush into getting a vegetable plot. Although they give immense satisfaction, vegetables take a lot of work and good conditions to give much in return. The work load for fruit is generally much less initially, and then again annually. Now, I am not against growing your own vegetables – indeed I love to myself – but they must be seen as a very heavy drain on your labour and a constraint on garden design.

To start with, the soil must be prepared and made weed free for vegetables or fruits. But for vegetables the preparation and weed control needs maintaining annually, whereas fruit can often be grassed down or mulched easily and permanently. Vegetables mostly need sowing annually, careful cultivation and harvesting from the dirty muddy ground. Fruit, once planted, is cleaner, lighter work with a little winter and some summer pruning. Picking can mostly be done from a stool. And even when we come to storage, fruits are easier and safer, than vegetables; the rots of acid fruits may make us drunk but are not as likely to be poisonous as the vegetable rots. Some fruits can be stored as long as root vegetables. Frozen fruits need no blanching whereas vegetables need blanching or they are little use after freezing. It takes much more work to freeze a pound of peas than a pound of strawberries, though admittedly the strawberries are a sludge afterwards – but what a tasty sludge.

FRUITS SCORE HIGHER ALL ROUND

Vegetables can give high yields per square foot if intensively worked, but given poorer conditions, they yield badly. Many fruits, however, will generally crop well even in sub-optimum conditions. Yields per hour of effort are infinitely better for fruits, especially if the size and quality are not too important; for example, when the fruit is wanted for juicing or jamming.

From the ecological point of view, fruit growing is much kinder, with no bare soil exposed and a permanency that allows eco-systems to build up. The flowers of almost all fruits are more beneficial to insects than the few vegetable flowers. And the crop itself, if unused by us, is appreciated by the wildlife far more than surplus vegetables. All sorts of insects and birds come to my fallen apples but no interesting or useful creatures thrive on beetroot and Brussels sprouts!

Fruit growing causes less wasted work and less damage to the environment all round, even in its production. Fruit bushes and trees are mostly field propagated, with only a modest usage of fertiliser or pesticide. Bought-in vegetable seed will have been grown with very intensive chemical applications. Vegetable seeds need renewing most years whereas fruit stocks last longer: a strawberry plant may be useless after three or four years; a gooseberry bush will outlast a Volvo car; and an apple tree should outlive you and still be productive. A walnut tree will be (possibly starting) cropping for your grandchildren.

As to children and vegetables; these do not mix and especially if pets also become involved. Now, if the vegetable plot is fenced off like a prison camp in reverse, it may escape depredation but damage will inevitably occur. Tree fruits are high and tough enough, to escape all except the odd broken branch. Bush fruits are fairly robust, most recovering within a year from accidents.

> ‘As to children and vegetables; these do not mix’

I'd suggest any couple expecting kids or with young ones to put the whole garden down to grass and plant fruit trees. As the children grow, the trees will be coming into fruit and soon be big enough to act as goal posts and withstand the odd assault. Once the terrors are older, then is the time to establish a vegetable plot, when it will assiduously be ignored by them. (Only fools, and the extremely cunning, can ever seriously expect much actual garden assistance from children regardless of the level of coercion or bribery involved.)

A fruit cage is another relatively child-proof option and soft fruits produce quickly with little effort once established. The cage is well suited to a children and pets scenario and after ten to twenty years, most of its denizens will be due for

Below: Yellow Sulphur gooseberries will hang waiting for weeks just getting sweeter and sweeter.

117

replenishment by newer stock. By this time the kids will have fled(ged) and a vegetable plot could very advantageously follow the fruit cage on that site and a new cage with new plants started elsewhere.

> **'. . . trees will be coming into fruit and soon be big enough to act as goal posts . . . '**

EAT YOUR GREENS?

As to vitamins and kids? Which is easier; to get a half pound of cabbage or lettuce down a kid, of any age, or a punnet of strawberries or a glass of apple juice? All have much the same vitamin value. We all need more fresh vitamins and minerals in our diets, but it is hard to increase the intake of vegetables – most of us will much more happily down a bit more fruit or fruit juice. And these are so much less work and cleaner in the preparation. I'm sure carrot juice is probably better for me than apple juice but I can make more of the latter more quickly and cleanly, so I do.

You may grow as much spinach as you like for your benefit, and some kids may indeed enjoy it with you, but grow apples and strawberries, grapes, peaches and apricots and you can be

Below: Where are you heading for a snack?

sure the little ******** will be helping themselves.

The other factor to bear in mind is that young families often move house and if this happens, all the work making the vegetable plot goes to waste. On the other hand, with planning, almost all the fruits can be moved or easily re-propagated to start again in a new garden. This is nowhere near as difficult as most people imagine, especially if dwarf trees and bushes were grown and a year's preparation is allowed before their move. Dwarf trees can also be grown in containers which makes much sense for the smaller modern garden.

HARVEST WHAT YOU NEED

My father is a retired farmer and one autumn day he was visiting. I said: 'Help yourself to apples as I have far too many and they're only going to be left for the hens.' I came back to find he had gathered up every half-usable windfall and was disregarding the surplus on the trees. I thanked him for his consideration and chided him for not taking better. But old habits die hard. To a farmer, the best is for sale and the family eat up the rubbish. Even though there was a surplus of perfect apples going to waste, his habit was to collect up everything usable and to use it, and to store and sell the rest. He had learned his ways in wartime when waste was a sin and indeed I caught the same infection. Certainly, in the first few years after planting up, my harvests were light so every fruit was cherished and every effort made to glean every berry. All were lovingly eaten, jammed, dried or frozen. But as the years went by the yields increased, yet I still picked every fruit and berry, froze and juiced and jammed them all – whatever the scale or even the need. Just like a wartime economy, all was to be gathered in, and over the years the stores became full of jars and bottles. The freezer became choked and each year a frantic effort was made to eat up the frozen fruit as the fresh crop needed the space. How silly can you get? So I have rebelled and now I don't worry about picking every strawberry or raspberry. I know I only want so many jars of jam and so many tubs of fruit and so many bottles of juice. When I have those I can relax about the rest. I don't have to make twenty

Opposite: A new sweet cherry is not yet as prolific as my espalier gooseberry.

Above: It's hard to beat a good pear.

growing but in the handling, from picking through to packaging. Apparently a modern sorting line cannot be run economically where more than a third of the fruit needs to be rejected – even if the fruits cost nothing to grow. Indeed, most of the allegedly famine-averting pesticides used do not actually save any tonnage of crop but merely protect its appearance. It's damned ironic that we pollute the planet and our bodies just to avoid having a less-than-perfect appearance to each apple – which we are then forced to peel to avoid the worst residues. Yet we could probably have eaten the blemish that all the chemicals were used to avoid. And don't get me on to whether or not cucumbers are straight enough to be sold.

six packs of apple and blackberry purée when I know I'll only use four or five, so six will do. Just because the fruit is there, does not mean I am under any obligation to do anything with it. Especially as, if I leave it, the wildlife will love to help out and the sight and sound of them scoffing is a pleasure in itself.

Now I understand that we hobby gardeners are in a privileged position and are not in a harsh world, as yet, where every drop of food must be utilised. When fruit is left to wildlife it is returned in terms of fertiliser from their droppings and eventually even more fertility from their dead bodies, so it is only being recycled.

Obviously I am not suggesting you do not offer your surplus to friends and neighbours and so on first, but if you want to save work do not pick it for them. And never ever process it for them. A jar of jam is not only giving away double or treble your hard work (growing, picking and processing are three jobs not one, as I'll deal with later) but bought-in sugar as well! (And my jam is made with organic sugar bought at a rip-off price.)

LAZY FRUIT CULTURE

Naturally things are different in the commercial world where, because of the supermarkets' demand for perfection, the crops are sprayed an unbelievable number of times with all sorts of chemical cocktails – simply because the costs are not in the

LOSING CROPS OR LOSING FACE

As gardeners we may be ashamed by the failure of a crop, perhaps, but fortunately it does not, at present, mean we will starve. And there is little you can do about crop failures because, unless you are remarkably incompetent or unlucky, they are almost always due to the weather or other uncontrollable influences. As I've stated, fruits are going to be produced anyway – the gardener's work really only consists of improving the regularity and quality of the produce and keeping the most obvious pests off. There is simply no point in going to elaborate and expensive controls 'just in case' for any problem that may occur – unless that crop is incredibly important to you.

To get it in perspective, the chance of all the apples on your tree being attacked by codling moth is low. By doing nothing at all you will have enough to eat, store and the damaged ones can always be used for sauce or purée, or cider. Hand thinning out the obviously attacked ones and destroying them will let the remainder swell and possibly reduce the following year's attacks. Hanging up a pheromone trap in time will prevent many of the apples being infested by destroying the adult codling moths, but it costs, at current prices, much the same as a couple of trays of apples. Sure, if you have a small tree of a special variety or you live on apples, then go to the effort and work of such active pest control. But much of your work will be uphill.

The majority of problems come and go with the seasons and we rarely affect the result much, except by extreme measures. If you want an absolutely clean crop it can be achieved, but the work involved is probably not worth it. Maybe a better compromise is just doing enough to prevent total loss or serious damage. Thus the effort of putting up a fruit cage or netting is well justified. But in general there is little point in doing a lot of work controlling pests that are not even a problem.

The danger is the attitude and advice fostered by those who sell chemicals and even those who sell seeds that are 'strongly resistant' to something that rarely troubles them anyway. It's like the old story of the gardener tying tiny strips of newspaper to his trees. Responding to a question, he replied it was to frighten the elephants away, and on being informed that there were no elephants in the area, was glad that his treatment was so effective. I have grown almost every sort of fruit, and as I must restate, the problems are usually seasonal.

GROW WHAT SUITS YOUR CLIMATE

Where you live is also crucial. With some exceptions, fewer varieties of almost every fruit prove successful in the UK as you move from the drier east to the wetter milder west, where few sorts of cherry do at all, likewise pears and strawberries. Though local varieties may prosper and some fruits, for example the bog-loving plants such as cranberries and blueberries definitely thrive more in the west. Indeed I've heard it said that all berries prefer it in the north-west of the UK to the drier south east. The same applies to every other country: grow what grows in your region. And avoid known offenders such as Cox's Orange Pippin, which although a wonderful apple is a miffy tree and a sullen cropper except in the most perfect situation. Although hope is a wonderful thing, do not give up much precious space to wild dreams such as a free-standing peach or grape in a cold northern area. It may reward you once in a blue moon but will never pay its way. As always, grow whatever grows well locally. Mind you, if it grows well locally you can scrump some instead and save all the effort.

GET IN TRAINING

There is most reward for least work in an orchard of trees left to themselves. But if space is short, then one way of fitting more in is by growing the trees as trained forms, pruned to a smaller shape and size. This can also improve the size and quality of the crop as more trees in total can be fitted into a given area if trained. On each tree almost all the surface can be fruitful but on a trained form there is no wasted internal space whilst bushy free-growing trees take up a lot of dead space, with almost unpickable fruit on top of the canopy. But growing trained fruit does mean extra work. The simplest form of trained fruit tree is the cordon. This is a single branch grafted onto a very poor growing rootstock, usually set at an angle and tied against wires or a frame so it can be longer, bear a heavy crop and still be within reach of the ground, or low steps. Other shapes, such as espaliers and fans, are all just dwarfed trees constrained to a few branches on which, with skill and luck, we can get a good crop. And of course they look good on a wall or beside paths.

Below: Really ripe fruits need netting against the birds.

Above: This trained pear is just ripe for a summer prune.

The pruning regime developed for fruit trees and bushes was intended to keep them fitted into too small a place, and usually as a trained form. Newer varieties, and much more importantly, dwarfing rootstocks, were developed alongside to help constrain what are naturally large trees. Over the years this has meant that many more fruit trees can be grown as much smaller specimens than before. Unfortunately though, our gardens have also got much smaller at the same time. Now we need even more restricted trees and bushes.

In the olden days fruit trees were either grown on their own roots or were grafted onto seedlings or strong suckering stocks. These made very strong plants that grew enormous and came late into fruit. Modern varieties are almost invariably much more compact and bear fruit earlier. They are grown on such improved dwarfing rootstocks that these prevent the trees becoming much size at all and also means they need a stake to support them when in crop. The effect is that nowadays almost any fruit tree will usually bear much sooner, and crop more heavily, if it is left unpruned and not confined to some trained form. Just

leaving all the wood on a tree is ideal, both from our point of view and its. With the modern extremely dwarfing stocks an apple tree will crop heavily when it's a year or two old and its head is not much bigger than yours so pruning off branches and shaping it to a trained form is removing fruiting wood and reducing yields. In olden times the trees would never have borne a crop till they were immense, or hard pruned and trained, thus they advocated lot of the latter. In terms of total yield for least work an orchard planted up with one hundred dwarf bush trees instead of ten huge ones may take more work initially but will yield more sooner, and each year the crop can be picked and almost no training or pruning should be necessary. Of course, it still makes sense to remove diseased, congested and rubbing branches to prevent a problem later. Unless you want them to have a trained form to fit into a confined space, only a little careful work is required and it should never be hard or you are doing something wrong.

Most of the time, as with shrubs, it is best to prune out soft growths in summer rather than leave it till winter when they are both tougher and grow back again. You can hardly prune immediately after flowering as with shrubs as you would remove the fruits. But it can be done immediately after harvest, and in some cases just before. For example, blackcurrants are best hard pruned so the way to manage them is to cut off whole fruiting canes and take them to the patio to pick clean at leisure, leaving all the space to the new canes coming up from the ground. Raspberries do not all ripen together so their canes are best removed once they finish cropping. The same goes for almost all berries. Gooseberries, currants and grapes are usually least work if pruned both in summer and winter. These succeed best as trained forms, and their treatment is much the same but on a smaller scale than trained apples, pears and so on.

With almost all trained forms the idea is to form a symmetrical and pleasing aesthetic shape from the main framework and to restrict all shoots and fruiting to stubby little spurs set on this framework. For those of you saying: 'What about replenishment shoot training for peaches?' all I'll say is this book is about saving work and not making it. You have to be obsessed to want to train peaches; if you want to then go ahead, but don't complain about the time taken. Be sensible and grow it as a bush in a pot.

EARNING YOUR SPURS

Fortunately the habit of many fruits is to form fruiting spurs on older branches which, hopefully, carry a crop. This is what happens on a naturally growing tree anyway. All that training can do is to try to reduce a potentially congested and randomly shaped plant to a more manageable one, with a few well-placed limbs evenly covered in spurs. For almost every trained fruit the principle is the same: the permanent branch(es) remains and each year the spurs shoot out stems. Some species flower and fruit on the old bit of the previous year's wood left on the spur; some on the spur itself; and others a bit of the way out on the young shoots.

In almost all cases, all you need do is stroll past nipping off the ends of these shoots when they get too long and start

choking the plant. Normally this is done in summer, pruning in two or three sorties from midsummer – doing it in three goes lessens the shock to the plant (But don't shorten what are called the leaders: the shoots left to extend the framework.)

I always try and do the highest shoots first, as this is where the sap rushes and the aim is to check the sap flow. Pruning causes the plant to make more of the buds that are left into flower buds and not vegetative growth buds. (It also lets in a lot of air and light to the remaining leaves and fruit, so ripens the crop better. It may even, as with redcurrants, remove a pest or disease problem at the same time.) The summer shortening is further repeated after the leaves fall, when almost all the shoots of this year's growth are cut back further to stubs on the spurs with just a plump bud or two left. This prevents the spurs getting too extended and congesting each other. A summer prune is not actually essential but greatly improves the quality of most fruit crops and saves work later.

Below: Raspberries of any quality cannot be bought, only picked fresh.

Above: Grapes are easiest when grown in a container.

GETTING TO GRIPS WITH GRAPES

The habit of most grapevines is to produce about a dozen times as many shoots as you can accommodate and the same excessive numbers of bunches of grapes, far more than can possibly ripen to our satisfaction. For decent bunches of grapes on vines grown in the ground, not only do the shoots need thinning and stopping, but the bunches need thinning in number by at least half. This sort of work is not difficult once

practised nor hard and makes a world of difference to the quality. Mind you, it still makes sense to do everything else you can to restrict the vigour of such plants as grapes by growing them in containers, as I'll deal with later.

LEAST WORK OF ALL

For the greatest ease of all and the very least pruning, dwarf trees or bushes standing in a well-mulched piece of ground are the best choice. Apart from remedial treatment these will need no pruning and probably crop the second year after planting. (They will crop the first year but you must be strong willed and remove them all except one fruit on each for identification. Do this in two stages, once immediately after flowering and another when the remaining fruits start to swell noticeably. It MUST be done before the seeds are formed. For almost every crop, the long-term gains from removing the small fruitlets the first year are much greater crops in following years.)

Up until now, cherries, plums and other fruits, and nuts, have still all grown too big to be either trained or planted into the average small garden without much labour pruning them back. Now there are many new super-dwarfing rootstocks for fruits and some are proving effective. Not all of them are compatible with all the best varieties. In some cases the top has to be grafted onto an intermediary which is compatible with both it and the rootstock. This 'double working' costs more but offers even more dwarfed trees. However I planted some double-worked allegedly super-dwarfing cherries in a very large fruit cage I designed for a stately home's walled garden. I argued for more height during all the planning and was glad I stood up for it. For although the cherries were certainly more dwarfed than cherries used to be, they still hit the ten-foot roof in the second year. To save labour, in almost every case go for the most dwarfing stocks offered.

CUTTING THINGS DOWN TO SIZE

Keeping plants small has been a continuous difficulty for gardeners. Many solutions for restraining growth have been tried. Very hard pruning in summer and or winter is still used. Ringing a tree by taking out a circular strip of bark from the trunk and replacing it the wrong way up (not inside out) has fallen into disrepute. And most arduous of all was root pruning where the tree was dug up and the roots chopped back. This last treatment can actually be very effective, but no mean feat.

Research has recently shown that a method similar to one once used for figs is capable of saving us a lot of work by keeping our plants small. Figs are rampant growers and their roots are very invasive and long, they are persistently good at finding rich moist soil and then producing masses of long soft growth and little fruit. If their roots are confined, these trees produce short jointed stubby growths that fruit well. Old-fashioned gardeners would construct a brick box with a thick pounded chalk floor. The fig would be planted in this, with enough compost to sustain it in the box, but would not be able to get large roots out into the soil beyond. Water was controlled to keep them growing but never lushly. Eventually small fine roots would make their way out and find some rich soil but for years these would not be able to swell and grow big enough to allow the fig trees to make rampant growth. The procedure was usually facilitated, as was ripening, by planting the fig against a wall, which also restricted the potential root run by half. Similarly, planting a fruit tree over an immense slab of rock or a brick-built pavement was also believed to encourage fruitfulness by preventing the roots venturing into the subsoil.

I found that stainless steel drum from a washing machine similarly useful and a fig planted in this was only able to get out small roots and came into fruit early. Woven root bags of a non-perishable cloth such as plastic or glass fibre can do a better job. Planted in this, the roots of even a strongly growing tree such as a walnut are restricted. Moisture and nutrients can seep or soak into the rootball and very fine roots can escape, but no large ones can form for many years. The root bag allows trees on strong roots to be planted in tight spaces by restricting their growth. (I do have my doubts whether they will keep working – we'll see.) These special root bags are available commercially but I've found an old woven coal sack will do the same job and I guess the same can be done with any tightly woven material that will endure for decades in the soil. I haven't found a way to weave one out of car tyres yet, but I'm thinking about it.

Car tyres may not be beautiful but they do get warm in the sun and throw back a lot of heat. I use them as a substitute for a wall. There is no doubt that a sunny wall or fence, particularly a warm one, protects fruit trees from frost and wind damage and helps ripen the fruits and the wood. I used tyres to build semi-circular walls behind my peach bushes. When the trees were small the tyres were close but, as they grew, I rebuilt the wall further back. It keeps off the wind and throws back much needed heat onto the bushes, which crop much more often than those that have no wall. It's also easier work than building a real one.

Below: A recycled washing machine drum confines the roots of a fig promoting stockier, more fruitful growth.

Above: An apple a day...

Apples

Apples are everywhere – can you get them for free and unsprayed from anywhere else? It hardly makes sense to plant cider apples, or crab apples as almost any others can be used to make cider or, when under-ripe, a crab-apple-like jelly. Bramley's Seedling may be a good cooker but it is very vigorous and makes an enormous specimen even on dwarfing stock, and what do you do with all those cookers? (Actually they make a very good juice for drinking or cider!) Cox is a bad choice as it's a miffy grower. Beauty of Bath is a reasonable apple, fruits early, and is quite eatable straight off the tree but the fruits turn to cotton wool rapidly. It is foolish to have a full-size standard tree of such a variety unless you wish to sell the apples. The same goes for most apples, they are so productive that the most dwarfing tree will amply produce enough for most gardeners with no work at all. Modern varieties, if planted and staked well, with a good mulch, can literally give you years of harvesting and nothing else to do at all. A whole tree of a good early such as Discovery may be worth having but, for the most use for the least work, a storing variety will give more weeks of eating and you wont' need to do any processing to use up a surplus. Ashmead's Kernel, Granny Smith, Winston, Brownlee's Russet or Tydeman's Late Orange (prone to biennial bearing so thin it) are all worth growing.

Where space is tight get a few bush trees on the most dwarfing stock and mulch underneath. In the larger garden get half standard trees (the branches are lower than a standard) on a semi dwarfing stock so you can mow grass underneath.

In the smallest spaces apples can be grown in pots but the varieties suitable are so limited that you will be better of with, say, an apricot in the same place.

Apples do suffer from a host of pests and diseases but they crop so prolifically when they are happy that you should rarely need to do anything. Putting sticky tree bands on their trunks will prevent many pests marching up and down and is worth the effort. Knocking off the little mummified apples when you can spot them in winter is easy with a stick and stops them spreading scab. Painting woolly aphids with soapy water or cooking oil may make you feel you've done something but these pests' attacks, like many others, look worse than the actual damage they do in most cases.

LAZY PERSON'S ORCHARD

In the ideal world we all will have as much space as we need. I'm lucky, I have plenty to play with and can afford to have badly performing trees just out of curiosity. But in the average small garden you have to choose much more carefully or all your work is wasted if the fruits are poor, non-existent or useless.

Most tree fruits are excellent low-labour choices where space is available and can be more beautiful than many ornamentals, but where space is limited they may not offer much value compared to other fruits. Those fruits that are worth growing in the open ground are now dealt with individually and I suggest those that will give the most for the least in each situation. Take it as read that – although these trees are to be grown in the ground, hopefully mulched and under a low-labour regime to avoid watering – in most places at most times, extra water is the single most effective way of improving their yields and quality.

Pears

A fruit that is even easier to have a glut of than apples and nowhere near as useful. They do not juice like apples, neither do they make a palatable perry easily and pear purée is not awfully useful. Their storage life is less than for apples and to get them to fruit to perfection requires some skill. So why bother? Well, they can be dried to make tasty winter treats but more importantly, a good pear is superb, one of the finest of fruits, and it just cannot be had from the shops. A Beurre Hardy, Doyenne du Comice or Glou Morceau has to be grown in a rich moist soil, well mulched in a sunny warm site, ripened on the tree but picked before the colour changes. Then it must be 'brought on' in a warm moist store, where it will be no good today, perfect tomorrow and over the day after. A tray of pears must be watched or you'll miss them especially as they all tend to be ready together.

Pears do best in climates such as the south east of England – even better in France. They are difficult in the north and west of the UK, where only a few varieties are reliable. As usual, it helps to know of successful local varieties. Pears are a little

Above: Although many varieties may ripen in the open, pears often do best grown against a sunny wall or fence.

choosy as to pollination, few even Conference, being reliably self fertile. They flower early so they may get frosted and there is a plethora of varieties, trained forms and pruning regimes to choose from. Luckily for the work-shy gardener, pears are actually pretty low in demands and modern varieties such as Concorde, Beth and Onward are good choices. As with apples, the least work of all is to plant bush trees on very dwarfing stocks. Dessert pears never do well growing through grass and must have bare soil or a mulch underneath. As you will not need to mow underneath, the branches can then be trained to grow closer to the ground and the extra heat thrown up from the bare soil helps to ripen the fruits.

Pears are easier to train in some ways than apples as they mostly form spurs with little prompting, but they tend to have a very upright habit of growth that has to be stopped, ideally by summer pruning. They can be grown as cordons and benefit from a warm sunny wall, but do not let them be dry at their feet.

Pears suffer fewer pests and diseases than apples. The only likely problem is a maggot that makes the small fruits blacken and drop off. If this happens, cut one open and see whether it is hollow with or without a maggot. Removing all the black fruitlets may reduce the problem; running hens underneath gets rid of it and a thick mulch allows the birds to scratch out the over-wintering pests.

Below: What a flush; the hint of yellow indicates approaching ripeness.

Quinces and medlars

These fortunately make only medium and small-sized trees as neither is an awful lot of use. True, the quinces are reliable easy croppers, attractive in flower and almost completely pest and disease resistant, but unless you want gallons of quince jelly or love the chunks in apple pie, grow them only where space is not at a premium. I guess you might be able to grow one trained but it's not commonly done.

For the large garden with space for a small tree, quinces or medlars are visually delightful. They can be worked with heads high enough to cut under with a mower so can be grown in grass as long as the site is moist. The Japanese quince with red flowers is poor value except for jelly but more ornamental and can go in a shrub border. It is tough as old boots but a difficult plant to train as it has an ungainly bushy habit. The medlar is a culinary or dessert delight enjoyed by only a few people who like this weird fruit which must be bletted (rotted) before eating.

Above: Quince fruits have a delicious aroma.

Fortunately these are very compact trees and can be fitted into ornamental schemes if curiosity leads you to get one. The leaves and flowers of both quinces and medlars are attractive but as fruits they need improving.

Below: Medlars are a strange fruit – but little work either.

Plums

These are never appreciated in the way peaches or apricots are, yet the flavours can be even finer. There are a vast number of varieties and they do not suffer many problems. Many an old plum tree crops every year, but more often it crops one in three or thereabouts. Again what do you do with a massive crop in the 'on' year? Summer thinning can help relieve the worst over-cropping, but more often bi- or triennial bearing is due to the flowers being caught by a frost several years running and then setting profusely when they escape.

The trees on modern stocks do not get huge but so far there has been less success with plums grown on really dwarfing rootstocks than with, say, cherries. The new root-bag method mentioned earlier may allow us to make plums more compact but as they do not like pruning and training much they are still best left totally alone to form natural bushes and these are a bit big for most gardens. In the past, some were

Below: Plums are a much under-rated fruit.

grown as herring-bone-shaped forms on high walls, but with a lot of pruning and tying in.

Basically you need space to have plums as bush trees on most rootstocks. And as only a few are self fertile, to have some of the finest flavoured you need several trees. If you can afford the space, plums are really worth having. Bush trees can be left alone: stone-fruit trees are supposed to be pruned only in summer, as in autumn or winter the new scars are said to invite silver leaf disease.

Minimal pruning is the ideal but very heavy crops break the boughs so if they're swelling to make a massive crop then act soon and reduce the number drastically with garden shears or even hedge trimmers.

Other than wasps, the only common problem you can do much about is rotting fruits. Like apples these can be dealt with by a winter clean up of mummified fruits. Maggots in fruits can be reduced by using pheromone traps but there are usually enough spare fruits not to worry about losses from these anyway, (The squeamish may not wish to clean them out but maggot attack does not spoil much of each fruit, which can still be used for jam.) Victoria is good but a ubiquitous plum; plant a Coe's Golden Drop or a Marjorie's Seedling instead and get something superbly different. Gages are round plums with a different range of flavours well worth eating – try the Early Transparent Gage or Oullin's Golden Gage. Damson and bullace are small tasty plums used mostly for jam. Damsons in particular are small trees well worth having as they crop reliably and suffer few problems and are useful in a hedge or as windbreaks.

Apricots

These are rarely successful outside in cooler regions unless given a warm sunny wall. Apricots are not so much work as a peach or nectarine as they do not suffer from peach leaf curl disease (see below). And as they fruit on spurs on an older framework they do not need the constant tying in of the renewal system used for peaches (see below). Apricots suffer few serious problems and are usually and fairly easily kept to a fan shape. The older dwarfing stocks do mean the fans can get quite large but with summer pruning they are not unmanageable. If thinned when heavy, apricots are most delicious, with a taste and texture far superior to those grown in warmer climes. On walls apricots need a little summer pruning and can crop fairly reliably; as free-standing bushes crops are sporadic in lucky years, as frosts easily damage the early flowers.

I strongly recommend you grow apricots in containers, as this reduces the amount of pruning needed. Quality fruits are reliably produced, more heavily and earlier, too, when apricots are grown in containers. They will need to be moved into a conservatory or orchard house for spring and until harvest but can spend the rest of the year outdoors.

Peaches

As with apricots, these are much more reliable, and crop earlier, when grown in containers that can be moved under cover. This also reduces the need for spraying; outdoor peaches MUST be sprayed with Bordeaux mixture or a similar approved fungicide

Below: Peaches are best grown in containers.

to prevent peach leaf curl disease. Even on walls, peaches and nectarines always get this disease, which puckers, reddens and curls the leaves, making them inefficient so that the plant withers away over several years of misery. Bordeaux and similar sprays are permitted under organic standards and should be applied just before the buds start to open and again as they start to open. If trees are kept dry under cover, the disease cannot start but outdoors it invariably takes hold if spraying is not done.

Early flowers get wiped out by frost and the little fruitlets, which are just as sensitive, can be damaged by frosts for several weeks after fertilisation.

Peaches love to be on a warm wall but to keep them constrained takes a great deal of repetitive labour. Peaches fruit on young shoots that grew the previous year (like blackcurrants). If you try to prune them like most apples you cut all the flowering and fruiting wood off. Thus you have to create a framework on which the old wood is constantly replaced by new and this requires skill and is a great deal of work, even with practice.

However if you have the space and live in a sunny area you can plant a peach such as Rochester or Peregrine as a dwarf bush. They will need a fair bit of space to grow: each year the fruiting canopy moves outwards and gets larger until it is just too big. Although clever pruning can be done, it's simpler to regard the bush as expendable after about fifteen years and start again. But if you want peaches every year then grow them in containers on the orchard house principle that I explain later.

Almonds

These can be grown as bushes in the orchard and do best if they are sprayed as with peaches – almonds also suffer from peach leaf curl although not as badly. I have seen some almond trees survive without any treatment, crop heavily and become quite large. It is said that although they are self fertile they should not be grown near peaches or nectarines as this makes their kernels bitter. With space to play with in a warm area almond make an interesting crop in the odd years the frosts don't spoil them. Unlike peaches, apparently almonds can stand neglect if they're in a favoured site.

Opposite: These almonds could be usefully thinned for the benefit of the crop.

Hazels

To train hazels properly is a control freak's dream. The poor tree has to be turned into a horizontal cartwheel of spokes, which then turn up to form an open crown of vertical cordon-pruned branches. Or you can just plant them up the end of the garden, or even in a hedge and forget about them. The nuts are a high protein crop that stores amazingly easily and for years. Which is good news, as most years the squirrels will take the crop before you even spot it. Hazels can be the most minimal work and thrive on poor stony soils. Wild hazels are small; cobs and filberts have bigger kernels. Although self fertile, they always do better if planted in several varieties so the old sorts are not suited to small gardens as they get too big. New more dwarfing varieties are now available and with the root-bag method these tasty labour-free nuts should become an option for almost anyone.

Sweet chestnuts

Perhaps with the root-bag method, these immense trees may be acceptable in modest gardens where there are warm summers and autumns. They suffer few problems but crop only sporadically, frosts can take their flowers and leaves off and

Above: Cherries are least work not in a cage: no work equals no crop equals no work picking them – get the idea?

they resent bad drainage. Sweet chestnuts are nice trees though, if you have a very big garden – well, estate.

Mulberries

These make long lived and huge trees. The fruits are very much like loganberries and have a distinct and pleasing flavour. With few pest or disease problems a mulberry is a good choice for a large specimen tree in a lawn, especially as the fruits taste better if left to drop rather than being picked. Not ideal if you also run chickens in your orchard as I do. The root-bag method may restrict mulberries to a size suitable for a small garden, which would be ideal for the lazy gardener.

Figs

A good plant for the work-shy gardener, figs are hardy and reliable and give great ornamental value with barely ever a problem. But grown free-standing or even on a wall they only crop sporadically, unless you are lucky to avoid the frosts and take much care with thinning the fruits and pruning out excessive growth. To get figs to fruit it is best to grow them in pots. They can be trained on a wall but it is ungrateful work in a cool moist climate, where figs want to grow rather than crop –

Left: Nuts are no work, if the squirrels don't get them that is.

especially if you unwisely planted them in a rich moist soil. For best results, remove all the figs you can find in autumn as soon as the leaves drop off. Just pull your hands along the stems and rub even the smallest ones off – left in place these may destroy any chance of a crop the following year.

Cherries

Cherries need no attention and are magnificent in bloom but I was daft enough to plant them as free-standing trees and the birds steal all my fruit before it gets a chance to ripen. By all means grow these in your orchard for the birds but if you want to eat sweet succulent delicious cherries yourself then they have to be in the fruitcage or in pots under cover, believe me. The birds have all day every day to outwit and out manoeuvre you and they will have your cherries, even eating them through a nylon stocking pulled over the branch.

Below: Unfortunately walnuts are only for the larger garden.

Walnuts

Like sweet chestnuts, the walnut makes a huge tree, though again some suppliers are claiming it can be kept under control and fruit earlier when the roots are confined in a bag. The nuts are so different and much better when fresh: the bitter membrane can be peeled off the milky kernel. With space, this is a very low labour crop as the trees need no pruning or pest control, except for the squirrels again. It does help to hand pollinate the female flowers, which are produced weeks after the males on some trees. Pluck the male catkins on a dry day when they are giving off pollen. Store them in a dry place then dust them onto the females when they open. I tie them in a net stocking and puff this onto the tree on the end of a long cane. For those with long-term plans, a walnut orchard is more valuable for its timber than the crop. The trunk should be beaten with chains maims the young wood, which is then more burred and distorted making it greater value for veneering.

Above: A fruit cage with a half dozen dwarf cherries is a wonderful reward for almost no effort.

LAZY PERSON'S FRUIT CAGE

Soft fruits and cherries are such an incitement to the birds that, unless you are very fortunate, you will get no crop at all unless you use nets to keep the birds beyond beak's length. Although individual net bags, old nylon stockings and sheets of old net curtain spread over the bushes will reduce attacks, the only effective preventative is a secure fruit cage. (This also reduces two-legged rat attacks.)

A cage is a serious expense if purchased, though fairly cheap if home made and once erected is almost work free – except in snowy winters when the net must be taken off to prevent damage.

However great the expense, it is worth having a huge fruit cage, at least tall enough for you to stand up in wearing a hat. (I used to have to wear a special smooth hat that did not catch on the net of my stupidly low old cage before I junked it.) The great advantage of a cage is bird exclusion but the expense does mean the plants tend to be crowded in. Fortunately, the majority of the berry and currant fruits are happy growing together. Although they each do better with more space and sun, they are almost all from the woodland's edge and used to dappled shade. They also all like a cool moist root run and are very content to have deep permanent mulches. This means after setting up there is very little maintenance work, other than summer pruning and picking of course. Leave the doors open in winter so the birds can scavenge for pests; you can help the birds by raking the mulches around to reveal over-wintering larvae and eggs.

Cherries

These have only recently become feasible for the average garden fruit cage with the development of really dwarfing stocks and double-worked dwarfing stocks, which keep trees down to a manageable size. They can be trained but it is less work to grow them as very dwarf bushes, pulling very vigorous branches down to form an arc. At least the new varieties available on these new stocks are mostly self fertile – the old sorts mostly required pollinating partners, with the honourable exception of the old sour cherry, the morello. This is much overlooked and is not sour but sweet if ripened fully. Every so often it also can be very hard pruned in summer, as it fruits on young wood and so can be kept smaller than a sweet cherry on the same stock.

Redcurrants

These are incredibly productive and willing, the easiest of all fruits to practice summer pruning on and the easiest to learn to train in different forms. Redcurrants have very few pest or disease problems and are long lived. My bushes died on top after fifteen or twenty years, but most have been reworked up into new tops from young shoots from the still-strong roots. The apparently ghastly leaf blistering aphid attacks are irrelevant: they do not affect the plant or crops much at all. Indeed, these puckered tips are removed a week or so later in the summer pruning sessions. The only thing is, what do you do with the fruit? It is only usable in moderation fresh and as garnishes, and too acid to eat in quantity. However, redcurrant juice does make other jams and jellies set well and gives them a pleasing tart acid taste, also making it useful in otherwise insipid fruit juices. Strawberry juice or cherry juice can be bulked out and improved with redcurrant juice.

Right: Red- and whitecurrants are reliable heavy croppers.

Summer pruning is simple; the bushes have main branches and you trim almost every shoot back by half to three quarters in a few sessions. There is little to choose between varieties so don't bother getting a selection except for the whitecurrant which has a different taste and makes a superb jelly base for mint sauce.

Raspberries

Another very easy crop and, with many varieties, you get two lots of fruiting if you prune half a bed one way and half using another method. Raspberries fruit on the canes or stems that grew the year before so normally all the old canes are cut out after picking the crop. Thinning out the young canes helps as well. Treated this way raspberries fruit in summer. But if you remove all the canes in mid winter, then most varieties will throw a crop the next autumn on the canes grown that year. This is handy as it gives a longer season and the late crop rarely gets problems with maggots in the fruit.

Other than pruning out the old and congested canes, raspberries need little work but can be tricky to keep weed free unless generous mulches are used. Be warned: because raspberry plants spread from suckers, they are best managed by being grown in the middle of a cage and not on the sides where the canes soon come up outside. All varieties are to be recommended. Maggots are worse in some years: mulching underneath helps as the birds clean up the over-wintering pests. Autumn fruiting varieties often escape unscathed.

Hybrid berries

There is no sense in growing true blackberries unless you crave your own and cannot go to the woods. Although the thornless ones sound attractive they are mostly not well flavoured. The hybrids such as loganberries are more rewarding and make a tasty jam. They all need similar conditions to raspberries but their canes are longer and need wires to support them. The tayberry is superb and I find it crops well in semi shade such as on a north wall. Several other hybrids are worth trying such as the boysenberry. The Japanese wineberry is well worth growing even without a cage, as the birds are fooled into waiting for the red berries, to ripen, which they already are. These are delicious fresh and can be eaten in quantity without pause; also the russet-coloured stems are bristly rather than thorny.

All of these berries need pruning like raspberries; cutting all the old canes out and tying in the new. In a cramped cage they can be exasperating as most of these berries are too vigorous. Grown without a cage and if you have ample space, there is no reason why they cannot be less heavily pruned; I have tried just tying in the new canes and only removing the awkward and congested older ones. True, the thickets produced could build up diseases and pests but they also provide wind protection, and they harbour predators to eat the pests. I prefer the hedge-like row of my berries but they do take up as much space as some people's entire garden, apiece.

Gooseberries

The forgotten fruit. There are still hundreds of varieties, in yellow, green, red and purple, big and small, acid for jam or sweet for dessert. Gooseberries are really worth the effort and can be grown without netting as the birds don't like them as much as other fruits – mind you, the wasps do. There are a few thornless varieties and also new mildew-resistant ones such as Pax, Rokula and Invicta, which gives them a serious advantage, but for flavour the older ones can't be beaten.

But as we want to save work, go for mildew resistance as it damages the tips and covers the fruits with a felt. Incidentally, although mildew seriously disfigures the plants and in some cases ruins the crop by splitting, often the fruit can be saved. I pick the felted gooseberries, soak them in ever so slightly soapy water then run them through my potato peeler, which is a rotary sandpaper tub. This cleans off the tops, tails, bristles and the felt and they are ready for jam in a moment.

Gooseberries need an open site so give them somewhere the air can flow over them, as this also keeps down the mildew. If you want a lot of one sort grow them as bushes on a single leg; this allows the air to circulate from underneath, and prune them hard, just like apples but more carefully. Prune hard to the old stems leaving little stubs. Although ideally done in summer, this is a delight for masochists as the leaves hide the thorns. Pruning gooseberries in winter is no easy task as the thorns are vicious and make it hard to pick up the prunings which it is not sensible to leave lying on the ground. Put down a sheet under the bushes before you prune and then all the thorny bits are simply collected together for disposal. From the gardener's point of view, pruning is best done in autumn when you can see what you're getting pricked by, but in many areas pruning can be left until early spring, to reduce the damage from birds that rob the buds. Leaving pruning till spring means the fruit buds remain protected by a thicket of thorns. It's usually bullfinches that do it and they go for plums and daphnes too. However, if you only want a small crop of choice dessert gooseberries, or want many varieties, they are easier work grown as single, double or treble cordons.

Gooseberries love wood ashes, so if you have a bonfire give the ashes to them. The only problem other than the mildew is the caterpillar that usually appears in the third year or so. Suddenly you notice almost every leaf has gone and on those that remain, small yellow and green caterpillars are munching away. They first appear all together as a load of tiny holes on one leaf, then they split up and chomp like crazy. If you are vigilant, you can spot this initial hatching and a whole host of the tiny pests can be squidged in one go. In bad years, the numbers can be knocked down and hindered with soapy water, then fresh soot, fine ashes or lime dust spread around the stem will stop them climbing back up.

Gooseberries are very rewarding despite the thorns. Their fully ripened fruits are even as good as dessert grapes but we are all put off by the hard green balls sold commercially; try growing Langley Gage instead.

Above: It's said that God gave us gooseberries for where grapes will not grow.

Blackcurrants

One of the most prolific and health giving fruits these berries are a must. They are also the easiest of all to prune. Plant them deep to get them to crop more like raspberries and all you have to do is cut out all the oldest stems and leave the newest. But if you are lazy and forget they keep on cropping anyway and you can have a hard prune every few years with comparative success. Blackcurrants are ideal for the fruit cage as constant pruning keeps them compact. They do like a thick mulch and prefer rich conditions so love well-rotted manure. If treated this way, they have few problems. Big bud disease is just that, and any buds that look huge by comparison with the rest should be rubbed off in late winter or early spring. Modern varieties are mildew resistant which may be an advantage, but I've rarely seen crops lost to it in favourable areas – and for blackcurrants almost anywhere is favourable as they are very tough and reliable. I've even seen them growing standing on a muddy mound in a pond with their feet in water.

Josta

This is somewhat like a huge thornless gooseberry and has a similar habit but the berries taste of blackcurrants. They are very productive and reliable but need summer pruning to keep them compactly trained.

Blueberries and cranberries

Except in regions with a moist acid soil, it is only possible to grow these in containers of ericaceous compost and by giving them only rain water. Then they need virtually no pruning and their only common problem is birds. Having several varieties will help pollinate each other.

Strawberries

These are probably the finest of all fruits but are very short-lived plants. Or rather they are rather short lived as productive plants they can go on for years but are only ever worth cropping for three, maybe four at the most. Strawberries need a new site

Below: Blueberries are easy to grow if you like watering.

every few years; this can be got round by growing in containers or by replacing or adding to the soil in the fruit cage. Alternatively, strawberries can be grown in their own bed and given a low roll-off net of their own. Often they are made part of the vegetable rotation. A few plants can be squeezed in anywhere and the fruits covered with jam jars, which ripens them early and keeps off most of the problems.

Plants crop better if they have all the runners cut off as soon as they form and usually it is better to get the plants well established before cropping them. Runners form continuously, and leaving them on diverts energy which is better turned to making flower buds. The hardest bit is taking off the flowers the first year to get better crops in the following three – this takes willpower. Or you can plant twice as many plants and allow alternate ones to flower, then pull these ones up when they have finished fruiting the first year, leaving the de-flowered plants to grow on and crop more hugely the following year or three. In any case after another four years you must have started another set of new plants or you will run out of strawberries. Preparing a new site every few years makes strawberries quite hard work. It can be reduced by using fabric mulches to control weeds and, of course, straw or even newspaper under the fruit to keep it clean and from resting on the soil which encourages rot and pest damage. Do not put the straw down too early but wait until the flowers have set – this allows the soil to give some frost protection as it is always colder above straw.

Although there are several ways of growing strawberries other than in the ground, they all are short term and hard work. Those plastic dustbin-like contraptions that sit on patios contain little compost; to fruit well in these, strawberries need feeding and watering like a week-old baby and, what ever you do, they'll expire about the third year. I built a very successful 'wall' of strawberries, which was not low labour but worth the effort. I used car tyres stacked in rows like bricks and filled with compost to make a long low wall facing the sun five tyres high in the middle decreasing to one tyre high at each end. Each tyre overlapped those below and plastic sheet in the bottom of each tyre held in the compost but allowed drainage. Compost was shovelled into each tyre and a strawberry plant put into each side pocket created as the wall was assembled and then one apiece in each tyre on top. From then on the runners were easy to shear off as they hung and the fruits were up off the ground out of the way of many pests and the damp cold. This produced a wonderfully early crop but when it came to rebuilding the wall, I decided to go over to growing strawberries under glass in pots.

Grapevines

I love grapevines, I adore them, I even enjoy pruning them but their vigour! They so want to grow, grow, grow that if you don't do several summer and a winter pruning, they will take over. The newest varieties are most worth trying; if you want to take on a single vine on a wall, then you can have some of the finest grapes almost anywhere the sun shines. Vines can be trained to almost any shape but the simpler it is, the easier it is to maintain. Of all the fruits I consider grapes the easiest to grow badly. Boskoop Glory has proved the best for me, but in soils without much chalk Siegerrebe will succeed and this has most delicious grapes. In the ground they just get too vigorous – I gasp at the old recommendation of burying a dead horse/sheep/donkey under a vine for 'fertility'. Grapevines need a parched poor soil and immense summer heat to perform well. Cool climates with rich damp soils make them too prone to grow and not to fruit.

I had some friends who were impressed by their vine's yields; they reckoned they were getting the most weight of crop per acre of anyone in Europe. They were, but it had almost no sugar in it. So the wine they produced was like thin dry battery acid. What they needed was three quarters less crop ,with all the sugars and flavours concentrated in that. Unfortunately, it is hard to achieve a small ripe crop of sweet grapes for wine making in a cool region without a sunny slope and a warm soil. It is also difficult without a lot of heavy pruning and training. However, if you want your own dessert grapes then grow them in containers as I suggest in the very next section.

ORCHARD HOUSE FOR SOMEONE A LITTLE LESS LAZY

In a book about gardening with the least work, it is hardly apt to talk about the most intensive ways of growing plants. But although it may be possible to occasionally get a harvest from some fruits with no effort at all, it is often worthwhile doing

Above: A temporary cage will save this crop.

some work to ensure a reliable crop every year.

In particular there are a few fruits that will only crop reliably when grown under glass or plastic. Whereas in the open garden we can often minimise labour by planting in the ground, it is foolish to do the same under cover. True, the plants would demand less watering if grown in the border but the amount of growth and pruning engendered more than offsets this saving. Also pest and disease problems are worst for plants permanently housed.

I have gone back to an old method that involves regular watering and twice yearly moves, but it gives very good crops so reliably, so early and so easily that it is without doubt the least effort in total. This is the use of an orchard house, which may be a (preferably frost-free) greenhouse or conservatory, used to shelter the plants at crucial times, but for much of the time they live outdoors. This is economical on space and heating, and allows many different fruits to be grown in the space that would be occupied by a couple of permanently planted trees.

Left: A ripe apricot is a thing of beauty, and taste!

Cherries and apricots

The easiest and simplest of trees to grow in containers; I use twenty-five litre plastic drums. I cut the bottom off to form a tray, turn the drum upside down and stand in the tray, first removing the cap to make the drainage hole. With some good drainage of broken pots and a rich soil-based compost I have grown gorgeous crops of sweet cherries and deliciously aromatic apricots for year after year, with only a little top dressing each spring and a dilute liquid feed in the plant's water. The compost should be lime rich for these stone fruits. They live outside though the autumn and winter and are brought indoors in late winter or early spring – earlier if the orchard house is frost free.

Although it helps to hand pollinate flowers with a small brush, this is usually not essential as insects do it anyway, but to be sure, use the brush. Little pruning is required, though thinning the fruit is sensible if you want good-sized apricots. The flowers are protected from the frost and damp and the crop comes weeks or even months early, indeed by having several of each plant you can arrange a succession, bringing each one in a fortnight or so apart from late winter until mid-spring. Once the crop is harvested (nearly always by midsummer), the plants can be moved out for the rest of summer and autumn to ripen their wood and have their pests eaten by the outdoor predators. Sour cherries such as Morello are most suited to this method, followed by modern self-fertile varieties, all on as dwarfing stocks as possible. For apricots any variety is good, but Moorpark is the most readily available.

Peaches and nectarines

Although you can often grow peaches as bush trees outdoors and get a sporadic crop, even on a warm wall nectarines rarely fruit as far north as the UK. And if grown on a wall or trained in almost any way, either is immensely demanding in care and attention, to say little of the need for spraying with Bordeaux mixture to stop peach leaf curl disease. If grown in containers earlier and more reliable crops are easily won. But to avoid curl disease they have to come into the orchard house early – by mid to late winter. This means you get a very early crop but it's harder to get a succession. One way round this is to move them from outdoors to a shelter that is not any warmer but offers protection from the damp and from curl disease but will not rush the plants into growth. Then they will need an extra move, but only if you wish to spread the harvest further. Bringing some of them straight indoors will kick them into growth and give you an earlier crop. Other than watering they need little attention, requiring the same treatment as cherries and apricots. Similarly, the most dwarfing stocks should be chosen; your own seedlings are generally far too strong growing and take years to come into fruit.

Grapevines

Vines can be a rod for your own back grown in the ground, but are more manageable when confined in large containers. I have been growing some in the same containers, and compost, now for nearly twenty years. True, I do feed and top dress, but I am amazed at their endurance and, because of the heavy pruning in winter, the plants are hardly any bigger now than two decades ago. Once the grapes have been eaten in late summer, the plants are moved outdoors and as the leaves start to fall the shoots, about five or six in number, are all cut back to about two good buds each. This removes most pest and disease problems in one fell swoop. The sojourn outdoors cleans the stumps and the soil, as do the frosts, and in late winter the plants are brought indoors when there is very little wood to inspect for scale insects and other pests. The return to the warmth jolts them into growth and the buds burst. Once the flowers are seen about three or four leaves out on the young shoots, I thin the shoots back to leave five or six of the strongest ones bearing flowers. The others are cut back hard or broken off. The growing shoots are loosely tied to a tall bamboo cane until they reach the top when they are wound back down again. Any side shoots are nipped off as they appear.

And that's it, other than unbelievable amounts of watering. Even hand pollination rarely seems necessary. The greatest advantage is that, although you only get say five bunches of grapes per plant, these are usually superb. The space each plant takes is minimal. I can fit half a dozen or more of the choicest varieties into the space occupied by one border-grown vine. You can even grow grapes in containers outdoors but then the birds and the weather are against you.

Oranges and lemons

These may seem like luxuries and will cost good money to buy as the plants are grafted. But they are valuable plants, especially for the conservatory, where their evergreen looks, fruits and fragrant flowers are all welcome. Oranges and lemons

Below: Grapevines are least work if grown in a container – I recycle plastic drums making a watering tray at the same time by cutting off the bottom, making sure to remove the cap to provide drainage.

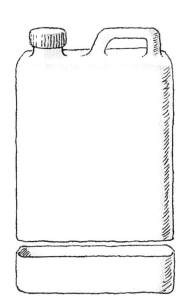

can go out on the patio in summer but must not be risked to the frosts, especially hard late spring ones that catch their new growth. They can be pruned back to keep them compact, but growing them in containers does most of the restraining for you.

Use terracotta rather than plastic if you can, and keep the trees in smallish pots rather than larger. Do not over pot but move them up slowly in stages as inspection shows the need. Use a gritty open free-draining loam-based ericaceous compost and do not bury the roots deep but keep them near the surface. If you have to use plastic pots, drill many extra drainage holes to prevent water logging and improve air penetration which the roots love.

Unlike stone fruits, citruses dislike lime and need an ericaceous compost and rainwater. They need regular feeding with their water at least weekly, except in winter when they should be kept barely moist and not fed. I use well diluted urine, comfrey tea and weed soup; you may prefer a proprietary brand. If kept very cool then the roots should be almost dry. Lemons are best value, especially Meyer's which is most dwarf, most prolific and easiest to root from your own cuttings. Oranges are impressive but poor value compared to satsumas and mandarins, which give far more fruits per plant, and usually in time for mid-winter celebrations. Best of all to my mind is the wee kumquat, whose fruit is edible, skin and all. There are many pests and diseases to bother citruses but most disappear when they go out for the summer.

Below: This is achievable with little effort in a Mediterranean climate or with immense labour in England.

Strawberries

Although these can be extra work it is worth growing a few strawberries in pots to force for an early crop. Good strong runners or new plants should be potted up in summer, the sooner the better. Keep them outdoors and bring them into a frost-free greenhouse in late winter. Very careful inspection of the plants and their roots should be made by tipping them out of their pots so that no pests such as slugs or vine weevils are brought in with them. Remove all old dead leaves. Put the pots up high on the staging, on boxes on the staging or better still on shelves right up in the eaves. The brighter and warmer they are, the better, for an earlier sweeter crop. Water them assiduously and on hot dry days mist them – but not when flowering or once the fruit has started to ripen. Hand pollinate the earliest flowers using a brush or you may get lopsided fruits. As soon as the fruits are eaten the plants should be thrown away and a new lot started. (It is possible with the best plants to keep them for a second year but generally they rarely do as well as new plants.)

Figs

These are least work in the ground or border but once confined in pots start to actually crop. They like a compost with lime in it but it should not be too rich. Little pruning ought to be needed but if the fig makes lots of long lanky soft growths, remove these in spring just as growth commences. ALL figs, including and especially the small ones, should be removed before mid winter as these weaken the crop after them and rarely do well them selves. Like citruses, the plants can go out all summer, as the fruits are seldom bothered by birds who do not recognise them.

Guavas and pineapples

These may surprise you in a book on saving work but actually they are low labour. Guavas, especially the strawberry guava, are quick and easy to grow from seed in any light frost-free place. Grown in large containers they make impressive conservatory plants and yield heavy crops of intensely perfumed fruits, which make superb preserves. They need little attention other than

Above: You too can grow one of these!

copious watering and can go outside in summer. Pineapples may seem like a joke but if you have a warm sunny conservatory then you could be eating your own, which taste far better than any you ever bought. You need the healthy crown of a ripe fruit, which is twisted out, dried off a little at the base for a week or so, and all the dying lower leaves removed. This usually reveals incipient roots. If potted into a gritty free-draining compost, the crown will root and, given a year or two and potting up each spring, will throw an amazing flower and then ripen a fruit, the size of which depends on how big the plant got in the meantime.

Keep the plants bone dry through late autumn, winter and early spring, only watering and feeding during the growing season. Once they have cropped, the plants usually throw sideshoots that crop with smaller fruits in succession; these can be detached to root and grow separately, when they will fruit sooner and better. If you want bigger, better pineapples, pot them up earlier in life into bigger pots and keep them really warm at the roots – they will even stand on a trivet over a radiator. Kept confined to a small pot on a windowsill a plant will still flower and set a fruit but it will be small, more of a pineapple chunk!

10 grow more vegetables for less work

Once again I must raise the question posed at the beginning of the fruit section; why grow vegetables? To do this well and neatly is a great deal of work, especially initial soil preparation, which it is foolish to skimp. The upkeep of a vegetable bed can be kept down with planning, but the initial setting up and soil preparation must be done well. With a little thought you can have some crops without doing too much work, but a vegetable plot can become punishingly demanding . This may be what you want – a healthy alternative to a gym – but the rest of us want to take it easy.

Go back and read the chapter on not digging; there really is no need to do it every year! Yet gaze in awe across any area of allotments on an autumn day, as men cast perspiration to the wind, working so hard to undo nature's plan. And there is really not much wrong with enjoying the physical effort of tilling the earth six feet deep all over, hoeing daily and watering every plant on demand. But for most of us it is not a matter of life and death to get the most vegetables per square inch and to achieve absolute perfection in the bits we are going to throw away!

There is a terrible conformism enforced by the old school, especially on some allotments, not entirely unconnected with the awarding of prizes for the 'best kept' plot. 'Best kept' meaning, of course, neat, unbroken (ie, unused) rows of perfect plants in a sterilised environment. Similarly, in our backyard plots there is the same self-inflicted censorship. You even hear of wives going out and buying vegetables because the husbands don't want their perfect displays of pristine plants disrupted. To say little of the tendency to boast of how many barrow loads of runner beans have been given away, or how many pounds of (hard, green) tomatoes someone got per plant. A little good-natured rivalry is not a bad thing, neither is having a show or competition to see who can grow the biggest or soonest. But, and it is a very big but, the methods and approach of these few should not have been allowed to dominate the way the rest of us run our own plots. Unfortunately they have done and worthy vegetables have been caught up in a make-work lifestyle.

IT'S WORTH SACRIFICING A QUARTER OF A CROP'S POTENTIAL YIELD IF IT SAVES HALF THE ACTUAL WORK

It turns out that most vegetables we commonly grow are relatively easy if you choose those suited to your soil and area. But instead we are told how to grow vegetables by those experts who grow for a living and not for fun or flavour. Now I reckon if you are like me, you'll put up with fewer runner beans per yard or not winning a cup, if you get what you actually need from the garden for less effort. Some tasks are essential, such as covering up the new potato tubers to stop them turning green and becoming poisonous , but it doesn't need to be heavy-duty trenching, as I'll show later.

Almost all the conventional gardening advice has been aimed at getting the maximum yields from any space, thus immense work loads and heavy applications of fertiliser have always been advocated. Little attention has been given to the quality of the produce or to the amount of effort needed. Many allegedly essential tasks are laborious and can be unnecessary or counter-productive. For example, the classic 'bending down the necks of maturing onions', this is still recommended in some books. It is alleged to promote ripening but instead it damages the neck's tissues where rots are bound to start later; actually they did it to make the bed neat rather than observe a higgledy piggledy state with some onions standing bolt upright whilst others have bent down naturally in every direction. Success will also be easier if you start with only a half or a third of your final plot the first year, and then add more. Taking it all on at once can be too much, especially if you are not yet familiar with the soil, site or crops.

When I first started growing my own, I wanted to try different crops, even compare different varieties. But what I was after was flavour and not to expend too much effort growing a crop most

Below: Medium and small onions keep the best.

of which I then gave away. There is no sense in growing for a record yield if less will do. And remember that whatever happens, the final result is nearly always dependent on the weather. In a good year the plants do fantastically and you have a glut; in a bad year, it's a wipe out.

THE EXPERTS' WORST TRAVESTIES: ONIONS, LEEKS, PARSNIPS

The experts have really gone overboard with some veg-eatables. Once-tasty crops are now made to perform outlandishly for the show table. The rest of us are made to feel inadequate by 'the good old boys' who proudly show off their rows of onions the size of footballs, leeks like tree trunks (and about as edible) and parsnips so long they resemble nothing like those you or I might grow. Indeed the latter deserve to be put in a special class of 'bizarre' plants. How can you compare a parsnip for the table with a show one? There is no resemblance except for the leaves and topmost piece. The champion is longer than you or I is tall, the topmost bit does look like a parsnip but the rest is just a very long bit of grey string. You would think it must taste fantastic when you consider the lengths they go to extract every last bit! Shame that it is just thrown away after the show. And likewise the leeks. What are you supposed to do with something the size of your thigh? Roast it with an apple stuffed in one end and call it a suckling leek? And the giant onions, each sufficient for a family for a week – sadly they do not store well. If you want onions to keep for the rest of the year, it's better to grow small hard ones. Now, don't get me wrong, as I've said before I quite admire the skill the 'grow it for show' boys display. I just don't like the way they are always turned to as the vegetable experts, when in fact they are producing parodies of the real thing by inappropriate and work-intensive methods.

GROW WHAT YOU LIKE OR WILL EAT!

As I said at the end of chapter one: 'it really helps to keep your eye on the ball', because it is not the giant vegetable growers who make the greatest waste of work; after all few gardeners slavishly follow their methods once they realise what different ends they are after. No the real waste comes from us persisting to grow crops that we never wanted in the first place. For this the allotments and their prizes are almost always completely to blame. You do not get a prize for feeding your family for free for the whole year, indeed you get a prize for not feeding them! Points are awarded for a good show – i.e. rows of immaculate unsullied and uneaten vegetables all standing in pristine ranks like a troop of soldiers for inspection. If some have been taken for food then points are inevitably lost as the show is 'spoilt'. But you may get a few points back if your edges are neat, paths swept, and anything doing less than wonderfully well has been quietly disposed of no matter how useful a crop it might still have given. And of course you get no points for growing rare or difficult crops but plenty for a replete row of Brussels sprouts whether you like them or not. There is far too much pressure to grow what all the good old boys grow whether you want it or not. A full row each of beet, parsnips, leeks and onions with their necks all stupidly bent down is almost obligatory, even if you never eat any of them. Put the whole plot down to sweet corn and strawberries and you'll be ridiculed as not a 'real' gardener! In their eyes that is. So don't be put off if your allotment committee has old fashioned pretensions, if they pressurise you to conform kindly agree with them and then carry on growing what you can within the rules. This is not an endorsement to have an untidy or weedy allotment but simply to grow what you'll use and not to grow rows just for the judging weekend or because everyone else does. And if you don't believe me about the waste go round any allotment in late winter and just stare at the rows of defunct fodder. All that effort going to feed the slugs and the compost heap, what wasted work!

Above: Chives make good edgings in the ornamental garden.

'. . . the real waste comes from persisting in growing crops that we never wanted in the first place.'

NO NUTRITION IN A CABBAGE

There are other factors affecting how we decide what vegetables to grow and among the most insidious of these are the descriptions in some seed merchants' lists. According to some claims, you would think that this or that 'improved' vegetable is so amazingly nutritious and packed full of vitamins that if you grow it you will look ten years younger, become overwhelmingly attractive to the opposite sex and win the lottery into the bargain.

Admittedly the claims for vegetables and the illustrations are not as puffed up and corrupted as for some of the ornamentals. One stockist's catalogue has conifers and roses of a blue you'd never see in a million years and other plants so covered in blooms you can't see the foliage; mind you, if you look carefully you can see half of them are wired on! This does no-one any good in the long run as disappointment is sure to result, especially from the 'new' run of claims for 'health-giving' vegetables.

It may surprise you but there is no nutritive value whatsoever in a cabbage, spinach or a sprout. Not while they are sitting out there in the garden. If you want their vitamins, then you have to bring them in and eat them. I'm not being facetious, but just trying to point out that there is little goodness in growing or possessing them or even bringing them into the kitchen. If you don't actually eat them, they can do you no good at all! But we are gulled into believing that if you have a row of new improved extra-huge super-vitamin-rich cabbages or sprouts you are going to be healthier. Yes, if you eat them, but if you can't stand cabbage or sprouts, where's the benefit in all that work? So, as I've said before, if you don't like, don't grow it!

If you think you might like a new vegetable but have never

eaten it before, find some and try it before making the effort of growing it. Bear in mind that the unusual is likely to have stayed so because it's probably not very tasty (as with most alternative spinachy vegetables); not very straightforward in culture (as with skirret); unrewarding in yields (as most); or has serious drawbacks (such as the bloat and wind caused by Jerusalem artichokes).

COTTAGE GARDEN? RUBBISH!

What a lot of distortion is done in the name of garden design. Don't waste time on unachievable schemes created by some armchair garden designers. For instance, cottagers lived on beer and bread and their gardens were more likely to be full of medicinal herbs than vegetables. Still at every garden show you see some cottage-garden design vaunted as ornamental and edible. Ornamental, yes; edible, barely so; achievable in practice,

never. The problem is that you can assemble a load of pot-grown plants for a show and make them look good, but to actually grow edible vegetables in the flower borders is almost a joke. (As are most ornamental versions of once edible crops, such as frizzy cabbages.) They can't stand the competition or shade and will generally be tough, bitter and unproductive, wasting your labours. Most vegetables need a place of their own, except for a few of the tougher perennials. Do not try mixing vegetables into the flower garden to save work; but for fun, why not?

Herbs are more compatible with ornamental plants than are vegetables because they need little from the soil, but must not be shaded or choked as they love the sun. But you can only use small amounts of the herbs in total. Mint is, without doubt, highly unsuitable anywhere and needs restraining in a bucket or it will take over. Chives are useful and make excellent edging plants. Saladings might be grown at the front of borders and even in

Below: A vegetable bed doesn't have to be a parade ground.

ornamental knot gardens or as bedding plants if given enough water. Unfortunately few salad vegetables are really decorative: they tend to bolt and if you eat them you are left with a gap. Salad bowl lettuces in various colours are the most sensible as they give most for least effort. To eat more and maintain the appearance grow replacements continually in multi-celled trays and plant in gaps as they come available.

Courgettes, marrows and ridge cucumbers can be decorative and add a tropical effect to borders but will swamp smaller plants. But they cannot be planted out till after the frosts and they get very scruffy from the end of summer. Sweet corn, peppers and tomatoes also suffer from this same short season. Tomatoes are more achievable than the others but will require a warm spot and rich soil to produce a respectable crop. Root vegetables such as carrots are unlikely to be considered attractive or produce large succulent roots in a flower border. Coloured beets and chards are worth trying, and salsify and scorzonera have pretty flowers but by then their roots are old and tough. Leeks, garlic and onions may crop amongst flowers especially amongst roses. Peas and Runner and French climbing beans clamber over shrubs and look like a bad attack of bindweed; they too have a short season before they become scruffy. Bush beans are good companions supplying nitrogen like all these legumes but again are visually unattractive and don't grow well among shady competition. Brassicas are very demanding and need good conditions to produce a decent crop – forget any idea you may have about growing them amongst shrubs, though they may do better with herbaceous plants. Ornamental cabbages are not very good eating but curly kale does make a fairly attractive foliage plant.

WORK COMPARISON

Some crops take more work than others. But there is a difference between work that is hard labour, such as digging up potatoes, and in work that is light but still time consuming, such as picking and podding peas. Time is often THE limiting factor for most of us and is, in effect, more restrictive than a limited space. Any large garden or an allotment can feed a family all the vegetables and fruit they can possibly consume each year. (But not the basic carbohydrate; you need another two allotments for

wheat or similar. And can you grow olive oil? Self sufficiency should not be the aim!) The total workload each year required to grow everything pales into insignificance when compared to the almost unlimited time needed to pick and store the crops and turn these into jams, jellies, sauces, pickles and preserves.

The same garden can provide very little if little time is spent on it but will fill the larder if but a few more hours are given over, especially if they are well timed. Growing only a few crops in quantity takes very little time, while growing a little of many different items is amazingly time consuming. I should know; for years I've been doing trials of all the varieties of each vegetable I can find, to see their differences. It takes more time to sow many sorts, and to write the labels, and then to keep the records, which doubles the labour again! So although I urge you to experiment and try new things do so in moderation, especially if you are a novice.

Below: Sweet peppers are less work than tomatoes and better value.

Above: Perhaps this vegetable plot belongs to a big family, or perhaps the owners will have a big surplus on their hands...

A good starting point is to write down all the vegetables you already are purchasing and which you could be growing. Then add up how much each costs you in a year! For example, you may well buy more potatoes in both money and weight terms than anything else. But they would also be a lot of work and space to grow, whereas garlic, asparagus or parsley may well be a big expense – and a better return for your labour. It makes sense to grow the expensive items you buy a lot of, not necessarily those you spend the most on. Tomatoes are grown by almost everyone with a greenhouse, yet for the same work (indeed less, as there's no deshooting) chilli peppers could be had. These cost far more per pound throughout the year and are a better choice for the family who eat a lot of them.

Many books offer tables of expected yields, but these cannot be taken as more than guidelines as yields can vary so. Some years all of a crop fails and another year you're eating it till it's coming out your ears. Still they are of some use to make a comparison of crops to help with initial planning. You must decide roughly how much ground to give to each crop and how many plants you can fit in. So I've compiled a table overleaf to rate the various vegetables according to their average returns

for effort. But it is only a rough guide; in most soils, in an average year, with a careful gardener, the same row or block will produce the relative amounts shown in the table, more with more sun and water, and none at all in a miserable season. Potatoes and runner beans and courgettes give you high yields for the space whereas peas and garlic give small yields by weight – but high in value. When you find by trial and error that there are just not enough or far too many peas, carrots or whatever produced from your first season, then plan to devote more or less space the next year. The table also indicates whether each crop is hard, moderate or easy to grow well and cleanly to the same quality as supermarket produce. This varies enormously with soil and situation and it is unlikely your plot will grow both carrots and cauliflowers well, for example, as the former need a light sandy soil and the latter a heavy rich clay.

I have assessed each crop according to whether or not it is usually easy to produce a harvest, bearing in mind its needs and common pests and diseases. I have further indicated whether each crop takes more or less actual time to be raised and prepared to the same state as you would find it for sale (though of course yours is a lot lot fresher). Then an indication of whether each crop costs you less or much less to grow than to buy. The biggest expense is the seed, some special hybridised seeds can be incredibly expensive so total costs vary much more if you save your own seed or buy the heavily promoted new improved highly expensive seeds instead of standard varieties. Not all crops are easy to save seed from and this is indicated in the final column.

Yield: for same space by weight: Huge, Good, Moderate or Light.

Ease: Will it be Hard, Moderate or Easy to grow it well and clean

Time: Is it Time consuming, Moderate or Quick to grow well and clean

Cost: Will it be a Good deal or really Cheap compared to buying the equivalent

Own: seed Will it be Very cheap if home saved seed or offsets are used? Does this requires Care, or is downright Difficult to do so effectively.

This table is only a very rough guide to judge which crops are best to grow for saving work and time. It gives an even rougher guide to judging the monetary value of a crop, as you can never give truly comparable cash equivalents for any crops. The price of vegetables fluctuates, with the earliest being most valuable

Crop	Yield	Ease	Time	Cost	Own
Beans, Broad	Mod.	Easy	Quick	Good	Very
Beans, French	Good	Mod.	Mod.	Cheap	Very
Beans, Runner	Huge	Easy	Time	Cheap	Very
Beetroot	Good	Mod.	Mod.	Cheap	Difficult
Broccoli	Light	Hard	Mod.	Cheap	Difficult
Brussel's sprouts	Mod.	Hard	Time	Cheap	Difficult
Cabbages	Mod.	Easy	Mod.	Cheap	Difficult
Cauliflowers	Mod.	Hard	Mod.	Cheap	Difficult
Carrots	Mod.	Hard	Time	Cheap	Difficult
Celery	Light.	Hard	Time	Cheap	Care
Courgettes	Huge	Easy	Quick	Cheap	Difficult
Cucumber, Ridge	Mod.	Mod.	Quick	Good	Care
Garlic or Shallots	Light	Easy	Quick	Good	Very
Kohlrabi	Mod.	Easy	Mod.	Cheap	Difficult
Leeks	Mod.	Hard	Mod.	Cheap	Care
Lettuces	Light	Mod.	Mod.	Cheap	Care
Onions	Mod.	Mod.	Time	Good	Care
Parsnips	Mod.	Mod.	Mod.	Good	Care
Peas	Light	Easy	Time	Good	Very
Potatoes	Huge	Easy	Mod.	Good	Very
Radishes	Light	Mod.	Quick	Cheap	Care
Spinaches	Mod.	Mod.	Time	Cheap	Care
Squashes	Mod.	Easy	Quick	Cheap	Difficult
Sweet corn	Light	Easy	Time	Good	Difficult
Tomatoes	Huge	Mod.	Time	Cheap	Care
Turnips/Swedes	Mod.	Mod.	Mod.	Cheap	Difficult

and the prices falling as maincrops mature. Local scarcities and gluts affect their potential cash value too.

Generally, though, courgettes, broccoli and French beans are very expensive to buy compared to the cost of growing them, while most roots and maincrop potatoes are incredibly cheap to purchase, even organic ones. Peas and sweet corn are time-consuming to grow but the bought ones are never ever anywhere near as good as your own. Ultimately, quality, especially freshness, is only obtainable from your own garden and the latter is particularly important for lettuces and saladings which rapidly lose their crispness, and sweet corn, peas and new potatoes. Onions, roots and maincrop potatoes may be better bought unless time and ground are amply available. Where space is at a premium, then the best all-round value comes from herbs, salad vegetables and climbing peas and beans. If time is very limited, squashes, beans and early potatoes can all be grown with little work or attention. Onion sets, garlic and shallots are equally easy and take little time, providing your weed control is good. Likewise for roots, if you sow them well in the first place.

STATION SOWING AND PROTECTION

There is something odd about the way we find ourselves sowing some crops especially, say, parsnips. I know the seeds do not last more than a year, but why is it necessary to sow all of them? You know how we do it: a long drill the length of the bed is drawn out and the seeds are emptied along it. At the end you find that you have half the packet left so these get spread back along the drill, doubling up the seeds. We firm it down and then wait till they come up like cress, only to then hoe them out to about a foot's length or so apart. The ones we hoe out are wasted, and those that are left fall over as there's no longer a horde on either side supporting them. Talk about a waste of time. If you want a row of parsnips, how far apart do you finally want them to be? So why fill up the gaps in between with even more that we will just have to hoe away?

Once I was on a gardening panel when a lady asked why she could no longer grow beetroot. She wondered whether her soil was sick of them as she used to grow good ones. Well, the other panel members talked about soil sickness, rotation, diseases, bad weather and fertiliser regimes, but not one asked how

Above: Beets get bigger with more space not less...

thickly she was sowing until I did. Yes, she was sowing thickly, each seed going in right next to the last along a drill, and now she was busier than she used to be, so she wasn't thinning them out. Beet seeds are capsules, so she was really sowing three or four at each spot. And how big did she expect them to get. Well, as big as tennis balls she replied. So I asked her to think about it for a minute: she was putting them in at about six or twelve to the space she wanted a single one to fill! It just can't work! (Funnily enough, I have often used this anecdote to illustrate the importance of giving each seedling enough space. At a talk in Scotland I repeated it as usual and at the end a woman shook my hand and whispered in my ear, 'I was that same lady.' Whoops!)

The point is this: more of the same seedlings are just as much competition – if not more so – than a whole host of weeds. Sowing too thickly makes work, as we have to thin them all out later. Even drawing out a drill is the first mistake, as it incites us to sow thickly. It is far better to station sow; that is, to make a hole at every point in a row or block where you would like a mature plant to be. Then at each spot sow three seeds in a small triangle and firm them in. Cover them with a plastic ring, cloche or at least a bit of netting. There is not much point in sowing to have them eaten off by birds as soon as they appear.

Once they do emerge each set of three seedlings is reduced by hand to the single strongest seedling. The plastic ring or cloche indicates exactly where each station is, so you can hoe in between with impunity even before the seedlings emerge.

Protection is absolutely critical for some crops such as beet and chards. You can sow these and look every day to see if they've come up, only to be disappointed. The trouble, is you look at, say, 8am, and the seeds did come up at 4am but the birds had razored them all off by 6am, so you never see them. A bit of netting or cotton stretched across between sticks, things that glitter and bang etc, all help to keep the birds off, but nothing is as effective as surrounding each seedling with a tall plastic ring cut from a discarded bottle. Cats and dogs can also mess up your work – wire baskets and wire shelves are very good protection for a bed of delicate little plants and though they may look hideous, they are only there for a short while. Likewise pea guards (low tunnels of small-gauge wire netting) for a row of peas are almost essential to keep the mice from digging up the seeds and the birds from eating the young leaves.

The alternative to protecting seedlings in situ is to grow them on in pots or multi-celled trays somewhere else and plant them out, still with some protection, after hardening off. This way you can be sure of getting a plant in each spot; it is in many ways easier than sowing in situ and the care of the young seedlings can be done away from all the pests and weather in a coldframe or greenhouse. Some such as beet and onions can even be sown in clumps of three or five if they are planted out with plenty of space between each clump, saving work by reducing the number of operations performed and making hoeing in between easier. Growing in a seedbed outdoors has little advantage for saving work but can give better results for brassicas and leeks.

It helps if you mentally group your vegetables according to their habits and treatment. This is how I categorise mine:

Plants that can easily be grown from home-saved seed: asparagus, asparagus peas, broad beans, French beans and runner beans, carrots, cucumbers, leeks, melons, onions, peas, salsify, spinach, peppers, tomatoes and watermelon.

Plants that can be easily grown from offsets, tubers or cuttings: chives, garlic, globe artichokes, horseradish, Jerusalem artichokes, perennial herbs, potatoes, rhubarb, runner beans (overwinter the roots like dahlias), seakale, shallots, tree onions.

Plants best sown in situ: beans, carrots, chicory, fennel, Hamburg parsley, Japanese or autumn onions, parsnips, peas, radishes, salsify, scorzonera, spring onions, sweet corn, turnips and swedes.

Plants best sown in a seed bed (preferably transplanted once to form better rootballs) for planting out: Brussels sprouts, broccoli, cabbages, cauliflowers, kale and leeks.

Plants best sown under cover in multi-celled packs or small pots: beetroot, chard, most herbs, kohl rabi, lettuce and saladings, onions, parsley and spinach.

Plants best started under cover in pots: globe artichokes, French beans, ridge cucumbers and gherkins, marrows, squashes and pumpkins.

Plants best started under cover with heat to germinate: basil, celery, celeriac, cucumbers, hot peppers, melons, okra, sweet peppers, tomatoes and watermelons.

ROTATE OR DIE

One essential rule with vegetable growing – and to a certain extent all other cultivated plants – is not to keep growing the same plant in the same place. It 'eats' all the available foods and leaves diseases, pests and toxins that prevent similar plants from thriving until some time has passed. However it is not important to follow exactly the rotations shown in books. These are only worked examples that show how the author claimed he did it. What is actually important is never to bring the same, or a closely related, crop back to the same bit of ground for as long as possible and preferably not for at least three or four years. And some crops are critical; brassicas, potatoes and tomatoes, onions and roots such as carrots and parsnips must be rotated or they rapidly get problems. Other crops such as sweet corn and beans are less problematic and can be fudged if necessary to enable the others to be given their first choice.

TWO FOR ONE: COMPANION PLANTING

There is much to be gained from combining crops, that is, mixing them up. When you have a monoculture of a single crop, it is easy for problems to spread; when there is a mixture, this spread is hindered. Mixed crops often do not compete so much with each other, so you can get bigger yields in total. For example, if instead of having one bed each of corn, peas and potatoes I plant the same number of plants of each but mixed up and spread over the three beds, then I get about a fifth more yield in total for all of them.

Some crops don't like each other, some are indifferent and some positively revel in other's company. This is further complicated by interactions with other plants, such as aromatic herbs. These latter give off smells that confuse pests that attack the crops but their own secretions can hinder crop germination or growth, so they need confining to the edges of the vegetable bed. A few plants such as French marigolds (*Tagetes patula*), *Limnanthes douglasii* and *Phacelia tanacetifolia* are so useful for encouraging beneficial insects and benign enough to be sown in any vacant spaces. But do not worry too much about complicated companionships, as it is really rather advanced gardening and although it has the potential to save us much work the techniques are still in their infancy. However if you are as fascinated as I am by such strange interactions then read my *Complete Book of Companion Gardening*. But certain tried and tested combinations are worth using in almost every plot as they save much work.

Potatoes and broad beans This combination works best for maincrop varieties of potato. When the sets are planted, sow broad beans in the same holes. These emerge before the spuds and shelter the latter's more tender foliage from the cold winds. If a frost is predicted a sheet can be laid over the bed, which will rest on the beans thus safeguarding the potato leaves. The beans crop and die away before the maincrop potatoes finish growing, so the leguminous beans give up their surplus nitrogen to the spuds, boosting their yields significantly.

Corn, squash and beans When sowing sweet corn you can sow Runner and French climbing beans in the same holes and the two will grow up together to no disadvantage and the saving of supports. You can also add any of the cucurbits – that is,

Above: Beans are legumes and enrich the soil for other plants.

cucumber, melon, marrow or squashes – all of which thrive in the dappled shade under the corn and beans. (When the European explorer in South America, de Soto, first saw corn, it was being grown in this trio, called 'the three sisters' by the indigenous people who had learned these crops thrived together.)

French beans and brassicas This has recently been shown to be a very effective combination for decreasing pest problems on brassicas, while their shelter helps the beans in windier areas. The beans being legumes can also feed surplus nitrogen to the brassicas, which are always hungry for it.

PERENNIAL CROPPERS

Without doubt the vegetables that are least work to grow have to be perennials. True, you have to make sure their beds are totally weed free initially and give them a good start, but after that you can have years of cropping with little maintenance at all other than weed control, which is often best achieved with thick mulches. The most important of these vegetables are asparagus, artichokes of both sorts, seakale and rhubarb. These are not only very low maintenance but the first two are expensive crops to buy, seakale is rarely seen, and bought rhubarb is sad soft old stuff compared to home grown. Perennial vegetables are also so vigorous and competitive that they can even be fitted into many ornamental schemes or used to fill difficult-to-work corners with meagre but work-free productivity.

Asparagus You do need extremely good weed control, especially to grow it in situ from seed, but then you'll get the best plants. It comes up easily from seed and crops nearly as quickly as bought-in plants, which resent transplanting. If buying in, get as young plants as possible, plant them as soon as you can and firm the roots in well, after splaying them widely but shallowly. Take care not to injure the buds in the middle of the crown. It can be mulched once established, but this makes the crop start later in the season. Do not cut spears for the first few years. Thereafter, cut every spear until the end of spring when you should leave the rest to grow on into fern. The fern needs to wither before tidying it up in autumn. Its wide-ranging, surface-running roots mean asparagus can only go where the soil will not be disturbed – in its own bed or even in a shrub or herbaceous border.

Below: Don't rely on the smell of the onions to deter pests, put the carrots under a fleece.

The following is a table of which vegetables can be most usefully grown with others, if each is given enough space. It also shows which ones do not thrive together and should be kept apart.

Crop	Good grown with	Does Badly with
Beans, broad & field	Brassicas, Carrots, Celery, Cucurbits, Potatoes, Summer savory and most herbs	Onions and garlic
Beans, French	Celery, Cucurbits, Potatoes, Strawberries and Sweet corn	Onions and garlic
Beans, Runner	Sweet corn and Summer savoury	Beetroot and chards, and Kohlrabi.
Beetroot and chards	most Beans, Brassicas, Onions and garlic, Kohlrabi, Parsnips and Swedes	Runner beans
Brassicas (ie. cabbage, kale, cauliflower, broccoli, sprouts)	Beetroot and chards, Celery, Dill, Nasturtiums, Onions and garlic, Peas and Potatoes	Runner beans, Strawberries
Carrots	Chives, Leeks, Lettuce, Onions and garlic, Peas and Tomatoes.	
Celery (and Celeriac)	Brassicas, Beans, Leeks, Tomatoes	
Cucurbits (ie Cucumbers, Courgettes, Marrows, Melons, Pumpkins and Squashes)	Beans, Nasturtium, Peas, and Sweet corn	Potatoes
Leeks	Carrots, Celery, and Onions	
Lettuce	Carrots, Cucurbits, Radish, Strawberries and Chervil	
Onions and garlic	Beetroot and chards, Lettuce, Strawberry, Summer savory, and Tomatoes	Beans, Peas
Peas	Beans, Carrots, Cucurbits, Sweet corn, Turnips and Potatoes.	Onions and garlic
Potatoes	Beans, Brassicas, Peas and Sweet corn	Tomatoes, Cucurbits
Sweet corn	Beans, Cucurbits, Peas and Potatoes	
Sweet and chilli peppers	Basil	Kohl rabi, Radishes
Sunflowers	Cucurbits, Nasturtiums	Potatoes, Runner beans, Grass
Tomato	Asparagus, Basil, Carrots, Brassicas, Onions and garlic and Parsley	Kohlrabi, Potatoes
Turnips and Swedes	Peas and Beans, Beetroot and chards	

Above: Asparagus is one of the most valuable crops yet one of the easiest for the patient gardener.

Globe artichokes These are best grown from offsets from a good variety but seed-grown plants also do very well. Do not let the buds come into flower the first summer, or preferably ever, as the plants may waste away. The flower bud is the treat we eat so it is best harvested young. Apart from covering the crowns with their own cut up dried stems and some loose straw or similar to keep off the frost, there is no work needed for these glorious subjects, which look majestic and fit quite rightly into the flower border as foliage plants.

Jerusalem artichokes These are productive, easy, tough and problem free; the tubers are just left in the ground till you want to harvest some, from when the stems wither until they shoot again. If their soil is likely to be frozen solid, cover them with loose straw and a plastic sheet so they can be dug out, but they are poor things if lifted and stored any other way. Once established, a patch of plants is hard to eradicate. They do better in a good spot but can be given the most unrewarding ground and they will still give you a crop. Just drop the tubers in a hole apiece and stand back. The plants resemble spindly sunflowers and can go at the back of borders, or almost anywhere else. If you want food for free forever, then learn to love this vegetable, as it gives the most for the least work – indeed you'll never be rid of it.

Seakale Seldom grown or sold, the blanched shoots are eaten in spring. Cooked , they resemble thin cabbage stalks but with a finer flavour. The plants are best started from offsets of good

varieties but can be grown from seed. After a couple of years of building up the plant, it is covered with a bucket in late winter before growth commences and the blanched new shoots are harvested in spring when about a hand's breadth tall and just unfurling. The plant is then allowed to recover and is quite attractive enough to be grown in the flower border. In fact an ornamental flowering form is available but it is not very edible.

Rhubarb Everyone knows how rhubarb survives in old gardens without any attention. It does do better given a mulch but after planting a piece of root with a bud, or a young plant, you never need do much again. Rhubarb even suppresses many weeds around it and the leaf discarded when a stalk is pulled makes a handy mini-mulch mat to drop on a persistent weed. Rhubarb is usually forced witha bucket, but to get longer stems I find an old bottomless dustbin loosely filled with straw even better. The first stalks can be pulled (always pull stalks with a twisting action; never cut them as they bleed and rot more easily) from early spring till early summer. After that they're too old and full of poisonous oxalates – as are their green leaves at all times.

Perennial broccoli Just like a small multi-headed sprouting broccoli only long lived. It may make five years or so but slowly gets too straggly and unlovely to persist with. Not very useful unless you adore broccoli and want to try every variety; it produces a crop from early spring.

Good King Henry This is an old-fashioned alternative to asparagus and is eaten in much the same way except the small shoots can additionally be eaten as a spinach-type vegetable when the leaves first unfurl. It is a very resilient perennial, coming true from seed and making a good edible ground cover for moist places. Once planted you can enjoy the shoots every spring for no more work at all.

Wild plants and spinaches There are probably two or three hundred wild plants that you can allow to flourish and crop if you are prepared to live on a diet of spinach, including cooked leaves of docks and hedge garlic. Although this is certainly a low-work approach, the majority of such foods are unappetising and few of us are determined enough to avoid labour to rely on them. However, some such as nettle tops and blanched dandelion leaves are surprisingly good. In fact, I allow dandelions to seed just in order to have plants to blanch, simply putting large flower pots over them for a week or so which turns their leaves yellow and less bitter.

Self sowers and edible weeds Once you have been cultivating any plot for a few years, you start to get fewer weeds coming up as you exhaust their supply of seeds in the soil. (Unless you have lousy weed control that is!) You also become adept at distinguishing weed seedlings from crops. At this stage you can deliberately allow certain crop plants to become self seeders. This does add a touch of randomness to the garden design but there is usually a surplus to choose from and some order can be imposed. Celery, celeriac, parsley, leeks, beetroot OR chards (they cross pollinate), chives, rocambole, nasturtiums, chervil, rocket, mustard, and edible weeds such as fat hen and dandelion are all relatively easy to leave to let seed and will soon be coming up everywhere and displacing other less useful weeds. Some you'd think would succeed, such as peas and beans, do not do well as the mice get them.

Herbs Perennial herbs are one of the easiest of the groups of edibles to grow. We don't need much of them by weight, we do require lots of small amounts throughout the year and they are fairly expensive to buy. Fortunately herbs are mostly reliable in the right place. They are almost all in need of a warm sunny spot with a free-draining soil and they really must be near the kitchen so they can be picked with little effort. A beautiful herb bed some distance away will rarely be visited, while a patch by the door will be utilised for almost every meal. If a special but distant bed is desired than double up, with the most useful herbs also growing by the door. And for those that you want a lot of, grow them as short-term crops in the vegetable bed or at the front of a flower border. Taller ones such as sage and rosemary are more difficult to fit in than chives, tarragon and marjoram. For woody herbs such as lavender and rosemary, it is less work to strike new cuttings every few years or so and replace old plants than to keep them pruned to a good compact shape, but do rotate their positions.

Below: An allotment is a good investment.

LAZY PERSON'S VEGETABLE PLOT

First of all, any vegetable plot should be slightly smaller than you want. You'll probably get the same yields but you won't have as much to look after. Site it in full sun and keep it far from trees, privet and leylandii hedges and other hungry feeders. Next, do not even consider anything other than a fixed-path fixed-bed system with the beds well dug initially but not thereafter (see chapter 5). Then consider everything I've written about which crops and how much to grow. Especially consider what you really want to eat. In many ways the best value comes from lots of saladings and annual herbs raised in batches in multi-celled trays and planted out successionally. This can be a lot of routine light work but is fairly remunerative . The main crops such as peas, beans and so on, take much more work initially but then are less work to keep up with than the constant replenishment needed for a salad bed. Still, many crops are well worth growing if you can but keep the labour down, so do read the advice on the packets and then give each seed more space and sow fewer of them. Do not soak early sowings of peas and beans as often recommended; it helps later sowings but causes early ones to rot. Remember to keep your seeds dry and cool, then most will keep for years – so you don't need to rush and sow them all now. (A dead refrigerator makes a marvellous rat- and mouseproof seed store and doubles up as a sturdy potting table.)

The following are ways different sorts of crops can be respectably grown with least effort, if absolute size or maximum yield is not so important as saving work.

Seed crops

These are the least labour crops in general as they are doing what comes naturally to the plants. Peas, sweet corn, tomatoes and so on want to flower and seed, it is their whole aim, so you will get a crop of some sort as the plants will ensure it if they can! Improving their conditions obviously improves yields but it is surprising how well some of these can do in poor soils, especially peas and beans. For all of these crops one good watering when you see their flowers is the most effective single way of getting more. Seed crops are either grown to eat the seed, as with peas and beans grown for drying, or the body around the seed, as with runner beans or tomatoes. The second group needs better conditions to crop well, as it is not so much in the plant's interest to make a succulent sweet pulp as it is to make good seeds.

Peas can be relatively little work to grow but are very heavy labour in the picking and podding, and blanching if you are going to freeze them. This makes bought ones look cheap, even the organic ones. However you cannot buy really good petit pois or really fresh mangetout or sugar snap peas. Most gardeners will have some supports to hand so should choose peas to suit them and not by tall peas and then find they need to buy new supports as well. Bear in mind that the shortest sorts crop lightly whilst the tallest shade everything growing nearby and need stronger supports. Sticks are tiresome to put in and more so to take out. It is far better to use galvanised chicken netting on a few strong canes to support the plants. Then you can sow in a wee slit trench and save an immense amount of labour, plus the peas actually come up next to the support. The bottom of the netting can even be bent back up and over the seedlings, shaped like the letter h, to protect them from birds and mice.

The dead haulm is easy to strip off, or burn off wire netting making it clean for next season. If you do not pick them fresh, peas can be allowed to dry and saved for seed or winter soups. All peas enrich the soil as they are legumes and, provided they are given water will crop on poorer soils. Asparagus peas are the toughest and more like a small cylindrical winged French bean but with gorgeous purple-red flowers almost pretty enough for the flower border; they are happy on the poorest soils and little labour and need no supports. Their pods are eaten like green beans when very small.

Beans, like peas, are good for other crops, leaving a surplus of nitrogen in the ground. They are full of protein and fresh green beans are expensive but never truly fresh. Drying beans – almost any bean can be dried for winter use – are the easiest work and least effort, as you sow them and forget about them until you harvest them. Green beans of any sort do need constant picking or they stop producing more. Otherwise it couldn't be easier. Don't sow any other than broad beans very early: it's not worth the losses, later sowings always catch up and do better – try it and see. Equally, giving each plant more

Opposite: Sweet corn does well near beans.

space means easier hoeing and bigger plants that are easier to keep picked. Climbing beans are no different except they need supports, but then they give bigger yields for the same space, if they get enough water. If your supports prove too short, just nip the tips of the plants out and they will get bushier rather than taller.

Sweetcorn is easy to grow badly and get poor results, but it's not much more work to do a proper job. It resents transplanting, and this makes extra work, especially as the roots need deep pots full of rich compost. It is least effort to sow sweetcorn in situ, two seeds per site in a bowl-shaped depression and covered with a tall plastic bottle cloche. Ideally thin to one seedling per site or give very wide spacings between sites. When the leaves fill the cloches, remove them on a still dull day and earth up the base of the stems. This holds them rigid and promotes more roots and bigger crops. Do not fail to water as this will affect the crop immensely. Sweet corn is wind pollinated so plant blocks rather than long rows and do not mix varieties as this can cause odd cobs. Sweetcorn will support running beans and can have squashes or similar underneath; indeed, these can all be sown together under a bigger cloche, say a five-litre bottle.

Cucumbers and squashes are mostly grown for the pulp. The seeds, which are really the most nutritious bit, get thrown away. Hull-less pumpkins have seeds with no tough skin that can be nibbled as snacks and are double value for the same work. All members of this large group need warm conditions to grow and early sowings are wasted efforts. They are all best sown in situ under a cloche – a big jam jar will do – and can be given better conditions and kept cleaner by sowing through a hole in a large piece of cardboard or carpet, which suppresses weeds and

> It is almost impossible for one bag to hold enough moisture to keep one plant going through a hot summer's day . . .

retains moisture. Winter-storing pumpkins and squashes need to be left on the vines to mature but all those that are eaten in summer must be regularly picked: if one is left to ripen then fewer will be produced.

Tomatoes and their relations Almost every gardener grows tomatoes but, apart from the very tastiest and earlier crops, I wonder whether it is worth the effort, especially when you consider some of the daft advice given by the experts. For example they recommend growing tomato plants in bags of compost sold for this purpose. This almost guarantees a corky patch on the end of each fruit known as blossom end rot, which is caused by water stress. It is almost impossible for one bag to hold enough moisture to keep one plant going through a hot summer's day, let alone enough for the two or even three plants suggested. To put that many plants in a bag is a waste of money and effort. One plant will give as big a crop as two, and more than three, planted in one bag. The bags are too rich in fertiliser initially and run out too early in the season, as well as being too small for a good root run.

So why do we grow in bags if we don't need to? Because the experts say if we plant the same crops in our greenhouse border every year, the crops will get sick. Well, sure they do in the experts' greenhouses, which are commercial and filled for most months of the year; ours are empty and recovering for half the year. Even if (and I found it took fifteen years) eventually our borders get sick, it is far less effort to dig out a trench and replace it with fresh soil every five years than it is to cart bags in and out every year AND do all the extra watering that growing in bags entails. If you have the choice, grow tomatoes in the ground not a bag, pot or container. (If you want extra-early crops, that's different, extra work and not for this book; pot culture can be effective if somewhat intensive labour.) It is barely worth the effort of starting your own plants for indoor growing, and only just for outdoor crops, unless you want specific varieties you can't buy. Indoors choose highly disease-resistant sorts such as Aromata and Moravi, outdoors go for small-fruited varieties such as Gardener's Delight, as I find these most successful.

Whether you start your own or buy them in there is no point making work looking after half a dozen of the same when you could just be tending one to start with. It is easy to root the sideshoots we remove from tomato plants as part of their normal care (to stop them getting congested with too many shoots) so don't sow or buy half a dozen plants of the same variety but get just one and then use these shoots like cuttings to grow as many plants as you need. Simply pull off the side shoots when they are no longer than your little finger, pot them up and keep in a propagator or clear plastic bag until rooted – which doesn't take long. The plants produced are physically mature, not seedlings, so will crop at the same time as their parent plant and will also bear fruit lower down, as they are short stocky plants compared to their lank parent – making them even more suitable for our cramped greenhouses.

Do not feed tomatoes; this will just add to their foliage and make the crop come later. However, do water them religiously, especially once the fruits start to swell. To ripen the first fruits, put a banana near them – do not leave red fruits on the vines as they discourage others from forming.

And as to supports; a decent crop will be very heavy. Don't mess around with bamboo canes for each plant. Drive in a couple of posts and lash a strong cross bar over several plants and tie them up to it with strong string. It's less work than a cane apiece and more efficient. I use secondhand scaffolding poles , which are cheap, quick and easy to assemble and will

support anything. Tie your string around a leaf base, never around the stem or it will eventually strangle it, then wind your string up around the plant, passing immediately underneath each leaf joint and then tie it to the support. Alternatively do exactly the reverse but still ensure you pass under each leaf joint and do not encircle the stem but tie round a leaf base. As the plant grows on twine the top part further around the string. To grow outside tomatoes means risking a late frost and then potato blight but they taste so much better than those grown indoors. If you use a frame for supporting the plants, then it can also support a sheet of clear plastic over, but not enclosing, the plants. This keeps off late frosts and the worst weather but lets the air through. I face the row towards the sun and in a way it resembles a football goal, with the plants set towards the back of the net and coming up and forwards on their strings to the cross bar. The cover over the top and down the back does not reach the ground or enclose the sides but stops most of the rain and the blight spores from landing and, cunningly, any rain is delivered to the plants' roots, saving more work watering.

Right: Sideshoots of tomatoes can be potted up to make more plants for free. Nip out the sideshoots when they are no longer than your little finger and grow on separately.

Other related plants such as physalis, sweet and hot peppers and aubergines are all greenhouse subjects with not much hope of success outdoors in cool climates though some people succeed in warm sheltered gardens. They are grown much like tomatoes, except they need no de-shooting though the physalis and the peppers can be over-wintered and cropped a second or third year when they give much earlier crops than seedlings do. They are all worth growing but do require considerable attention initially to keep down plagues of red spider mites and aphids. Peppers, especially hot ones, are very good value even if you buy in the plants to save work. All of these only crop well in sunny seasons and are best grown in a large pot so they can be kept up on the warm staging.

Leaf and bud crops

These are easy to grow but require more work if they are to be succulent. Plants want to grow and generally more leaves and bigger ones indicate a vigorous plant. If we wish to eat the leaves, they need to be grown fairly rapidly or they tend to be tough and bitter. Blanching the leaves by excluding light can reduce bitterness. It can be done by covering a plant with a pot, by tying up the leaves, as with a Cos lettuce, or by nature, where pale leaves form inside the swollen buds of cabbages and sprouts. A broccoli or cauliflower is an abnormal enormous mass of swollen flower buds, so it is not surprising that really good conditions are needed for success with such highly bred plants. But most of the other leaf crops are fairly easy and will cope with some shade. Their biggest problem is getting dry and bitter, so don't try and save work on watering. Bird damage is significant so all the usual scares need utilising, especially while the seedlings are small. Sacrificial crops of bird snacks such as beetroot and lettuce will keep the birds off tougher crops such as brassicas. Shredding spare plants and damaged leaves and sprinkling these around the crops will fob off the slugs and snails, which go for wilting foliage first.

Lettuces and other bland saladings. There are few crops for which a rich, well-dug soil is essential but these soft succulent plants will be far better off for your effort. Only a small bed needs preparing each year, not the whole garden. Lettuces are

Below: A plastic flysheet can improve the chances for tomatoes.

Above: Plum tomatoes are good for cooking.

not difficult and there is a plethora of varieties for indoors and out and all seasons. The least labour comes from the cut-and-come again sorts, those with frilly or oak leaves seem to do best. It is least work to sow a small number of lettuces every couple of weeks in multi-celled trays or small pots, to thin these to singletons and plant them out where and when space becomes available.

Other similar leaf crops and mild annual herbs that can be used in salads are also least work treated the same way. Most can be sown as little clusters and don't need to be thinned to singletons, save for endives and chicories, which get as big as lettuces. It is least effort to start the following off in small batches every few weeks; rocket, chervil, dill, lamb's lettuce (*Valerianella*), miner's lettuce (*Claytonia*), spring onions, radishes (if you really like them), pak choi and mustards. Summer savory and parsley need only a couple of sowings early in the season as these crop for longer.

Spinaches. True spinach is determined to bolt under almost anything other than perfect conditions and timing. It is only

successful if sown in situ and really ought to be sown in weekly batches to hit the right window. It is truly a lot of work to sow and gather. The New Zealand spinach makes a bigger plant for less effort and stands better, but does not taste the same. Likewise many other alternatives such as leaf beets and chards are not as tasty but can be cooked in the same way and are much less effort to grow well. Bird protection is essential while plants are young.

Brassicas. These are natives of disturbed chalky ground and really prefer a moist rich soil to do well. However, given enough space the majority will do fairly well in most soils. They are best grown in a seedbed, lifted once to break their taproot (which promotes the formation of a more fibrous rootball) and replanted, watered, then transplanted to their final site when they are strong little plants. If the taproot is not broken you find you get few side roots and when when transplanted such plants fail to take as well and bolt more easily. If you are too lazy to lift and replant the first time you can get away with cutting the taproots in situ; with a sharp knife slice under the wee plants at an angle so you sever the taproots about a finger's thickness or so deep, water them well for about two weeks to develop their rootballs well before transplanting. They can be grown in cells or pots but need planting out sooner than other crops as they resent being cramped. Don't even consider using cells for cauliflowers or broccoli; these are least work station-sown in situ under a mini-cloche. Caterpillars are the biggest problem and can be kept off by growing brassicas under fine netting or fleece. It is not a lot of work to grow cabbages, they are the easiest of this family. When collecting a cabbage for the table that is much bigger than your immediate requirements, do not cut the whole head off. Instead, cut off a thick slice or chunk and cover the remainder with a sheet of foil or a plastic bag. Left on its roots the remainder of the cabbage will keep much better than in your refrigerator. You can also pull cabbages up by the roots and hang them upside down in a cool place where they will keep for weeks or even months in winter. But this may be wasteful, instead, once one has been harvested, do not pull up the root but cut a cross in the stump of the stem. In most cases, you will then get a bonus crop of four or so smaller, looser cabbages. If you persist, you can get several flushes of growth from one stump, and sucker-like shoots coming from the base. These can be detached and grown on to crop in their own right and are often less work and quicker than sowing more seed.

Root crops

These are mostly biennials, plants that grow one year to flower and seed the next, and we want to eat their storage organs. Generally they are easy enough to grow and, given reasonable conditions and space, will usually give a fair crop for not too much labour, except in the lifting. This can be pleasant treasure hunting or a miserable muddy game extricating parsnips in the depths of winter. Root crops can be remarkably little work but may fail by bolting into flower if they receive a check in growth, the worst sin is to sow too thickly!

Beets and chards These are little effort to grow as long as you protect them while young from birds that razor off the small leaves. They are easily planted out from cells and can be multi-sown in groups of three to five. Chards are usually eaten as leaf and stem crops but are so similar to beet they may be considered to need much the same treatment. Both are happiest in a moist soil and need little effort to grow well.

Kohlrabi, turnips and swedes All closely related to the brassicas, these need a rich moist soil with some lime to thrive. They are bothered by flea beetle when small if not kept moist but otherwise, fairly trouble free. They can be cell grown but are best sown thinly in situ and forgotten about till harvest.

Carrots, parsnips, hamburg parsley, salsify and scorzonera All these roots are similar in that they do best sown thinly and in uniform soil with no clods, stones or lumps of manure. In fact, they can be sown broadcast on top of a rock hard bed; if covered and firmed well with extra soil, they will germinate and drive strong roots straight down. The earliest sowings may fail from cold but if they succeed they can often do very well despite later droughts as their roots follow the dropping water table down. Most of these root crops suffer badly from carrot root fly; this is best kept away by sowing and growing under a fine net or fleece to exclude the pest.

Onions, leeks, shallots and garlic. These can be fitted in amongst the ornamentals in the flower bed to decorative advantage and if left to flower are quite attractive. All are members of the Allium genus. Most will do in poorer soils but need full sun. Leeks need rich moist conditions to to get any size. Planting bought-in sets is expensive; it is much cheaper and not hard to save some of the healthiest average-sized harvested sets of onions and shallots to plant the following year. Keep them in a cool dry place and plant the garlic in autumn and the shallots in late winter. Onions and leeks from seed are not hard work and can be started in multi-celled trays or pots, but do require some delicacy when planting out. Autumn-sown onions have to be sown in situ, require much careful weeding, but give a valuable early crop. They are terribly damaged in a mild autumn by slugs and I've found one variety, Buffalo, is far more palatable to them than the Japanese sorts mostly sown in autumn. Rather than avoiding Buffalo, I mix it with the other sorts, then the slugs select it out and leave the others relatively unmolested and merely thin the rows for me. These Alliums all loathe damage and should not be hoed between but hand weeded only. Once they are ripening, leave the weeds anyway as they help the crop ripen off; by taking up moisture and nitrogen the weeds prevent the maturing crop from starting into growth again.

Onion and shallot sets need to be grown on the surface so are often disturbed by birds or worms. They should be held in place with a handful of sand or soil, which is washed away by rain and can be reduced or brushed away to leave the set standing proud (buried deeply, onions form thick necks and do not store well). Alternatively start them in cells and plant them out once the roots have grown to hold the plants down but again be careful to keep the wee bulbs proud of the surrounding soil . Do not try to just put the sets in and leave them or you will be re-setting your sets at least three or four times, believe me. And do not push the sets into hard soil as it damages their basal plate. In hard soil, dib a wee hole first. A dusting of wood ashes discourages worms from attacking newly planted sets and is good for the onions. Never bend onion necks down 'to aid ripening' as this causes rots. Instead, lift the onions and store them in a dry airy place. Do not try tying them together but store them in small net bags or old tights hanging in a dry breeze. Dig up garlic before the stems wither or you won't be able to find them. If left in situ, garlic multiplies, making a mass

Right: Sieving compost is light work if it's dry.

of small bulbs the following year. Leeks also make offsets which can be transplanted and so do some varieties of onions, which then become shallots of a sort. Onions that are bolting can have their heads nipped off – then they will usually form inferior small onions beside the bolted bulb if the season is long enough; thse small sets should be used up as they do not store well.

Potatoes. Only a workaholic grows all their own maincrop potatoes. It can be a lot of effort to do the job as advised with all the trenching and earthing up required. Of course, if you just plant a potato and leave it you'll get a crop but many of the tubers will have seen the light, greened and gone poisonous. Instead of earthing up with soil you can use mulch. I use thin layers of grass clippings applied each week, after all, you've got to put them somewhere and it saves work to put them where they're useful. These can be interlaced with newspaper to stop the birds scratching them aside. Indeed anything laid on top of the soil keeps it moister, keeps the sun off and protects the tubers.

Crops can be raised by planting through holes in old carpet, cardboard or black plastic, but unfortunately they then tend to be more badly attacked by pests. I find a grass clipping mulch works well and enriches the soil at the same time as saving all that trenching. Mind you, if you want the best yields of potatoes, then loosen the soil with a good digging, or follow a crop of roots such as carrots which have broken up the soil. As for most crops, one good watering when you see the flowers will multiply yields more than anything else you can do.

If you want fewer but bigger maincrop potatoes, do not leave all the sprouts on the sets, as seed potatoes are called, but reduce them to two or three before planting. To keep scab disease away, mix some grass clippings into the soil around the sets.

Chitting potatoes involves putting them in a tray in a light frost-free place for several weeks before planting. It is essential to sit them rose-end (lots of 'eyes' in it) upmost. Planting them the other way up (the haulm end where a wee bit of 'root' was joining it to the parent), is detrimental. Chitting is only really useful for earlies as it gives a quicker crop by fooling them into growth out of the ground first. (Do not remove any sprouts from these as you want as many small tubers as possible with earlies.) Chitting can decrease yields if done too long before planting or if the chitted sets go into very cold soil, and it is of little use for maincrops which need the longest period of growth in the ground possible.

Deeper planting of maincrop sets gives bigger yields but makes the extrication laborious. I should know, I planted some King Edward's, which are well known to like deep planting, at various depths to a couple of feet. Although the deepest took a long time to emerge, they made the strongest longest-lived plants with the highest yield. But it would have been less work to carry them from afar than getting them up from that deep down.

An alternative for gardeners without much ground is to grow potatoes in a barrel. Start with a layer of compost and one set of a maincrop potato. Once the haulm reaches the top of the barrel,

Below: Potatoes on the left are for immediate consumption, on the right for storage and in the tray for next year's seed.

fill up in two or three stages with more compost, watering regularly as well. Competitions have produced enormous yields from one set by this method. I use cut car tyres turned inside out to make the container and so can add more rings and compost as the haulm grows. Of course, early potatoes can be grown in pots and containers in any light frost-free place but the yields for the efforts are low. However, if you have a warm conservatory or similar, then planting a couple of pots of an early such as Rocket in mid-winter can give a dish of new potatoes by the beginning of spring when everyone else is just planting theirs.

Less work is to grow earlies in situ but to get them a bit earlier by pre-warming the soil. Cover it with soot or black plastic before planting, and grow the crop under a sheet of clear plastic supported on sticks and cover it over with a blanket at night. Potatoes crop earlier with bare soil, so mulches are most use in dry areas for maincrops and not much use for earlies – mulching these makes them later. To save worry about blight, which blackens and destroys the foliage then runs down the stems to rot the tubers as well, it is a good idea to grow only earlies and second earlies. Although these give light crops, they do so before blight usually appears. Earlies and second earlies crop quickly not heavily, and many sorts store just as well as main crops. A light early crop can be less wasted effort than a potentially bigger but blight-ruined maincrop. And it may be worth putting up with a later crop of earlies if it saves a lot of work and still comes in time to avoid the blight. If it does appear (all the foliage blackens, rots, stinks and the stems get brown-black streaks running down them), cut off the haulm at ground level and dispose of it. Leave the crop in the ground for a fortnight before digging it up and by then most spores should have broken down. Do not store any potatoes with ruddy stains to the flesh but reject and dispose of them immediately.

I have found that autumn planting potatoes is lighter easier work and shifts the load from the busy days of spring to the relaxed days of autumn. I select the seed potatoes at the same time as digging the harvest in early autumn while the soil is still dryish (spuds dug from wet soil do not keep well). I plant the sets, rose end up, in their new sites, deeper than my fingers reach, and firm them in really well. Then I cover the whole bed over with leaves and loose straw as deep as my knees. As long

Above: If you have no ground you can still grow record crops of potatoes in a barrel.

as the winter is not incredibly wet and warm, or incredibly cold, then ninety per cent of the sets survive and grow and crop with no attention whatsoever till harvest. True the yields are late and light, but it is so much less work than the 'proper' method and the work is much pleasanter in the warmth of late autumn than in the rush of a cold spring.

Sweet potatoes. I have grown these for years. Ideally they need to be grown in containers off the ground, under glass or plastic, but newer varieties will crop outdoors if grown under a sheet of clear plastic supported on sticks. The tips of the shoots can be rooted in summer to over-winter like fuchsia cuttings. But it's less work to buy them in as they're now sold commercially. Keep the foliage and stems up off the ground on netting or string to stop adventitious rooting, which wastes the plant's energy.

11

encouraging wildlife

(and getting it to do the work)

In many books this chapter would be all about pest control, but that is part of an old way of thinking. Ideally our gardens would have no pests, but then they would have no song birds either. A garden is not a place but a collection of many different plants and the multitude of creatures associated with each. Given time the various pests, predators and parasites all come to a balance – but this may not be in time to save our crops or flowers! Our aim as gardeners is to shift the balance, so we get what we are after without having to fight nature for it. Ideally, we work with her and coax the various creatures to do our bidding. Or rather to find out how, by achieving their own ends, they can help promote ours.

WILDLIFE AND THE WORK IT'S ALREADY SAVING YOU

Wild creatures in the garden are already creating much of its fertility for free. Originally it all comes from the sun, but without the animal kingdom breaking down vegetable material, the plant world would be much impoverished. Living creatures create high-grade plant food such as droppings from lower-grade plant material, or other animals. Consider just the extra fertility created by a family of songbirds; the feathers they moult, the eggshells, the fledgling who doesn't make it, the droppings from each of these every day. Add all these up for a year and you get the equivalent of a big bag of fertiliser and it's distributed evenly for you (everything that drops on the car is wasted but the rest is all recycled).

All little creatures produce droppings and it is these that feed the plants. The more creatures, the more fertile the soil. So even great numbers of pests can be seen not as a problem but a source of present and future fertility. The trick is in getting the balance right, so we get our crops and flowers despite the presence of pests. And all animal life, even pests, give off carbon dioxide all our plants need to grow. Although carbon dioxide is in general excess because of car exhaust etc, it is in short supply beside growing crops, which rapidly extract it all from the air. All the various creatures you can encourage in a garden make it more bounteous and, with cunning, they will keep each other in check and therefore do much of the pest control for us. Indeed, for many years I've done almost no direct control myself – my little friends do it all for me (slug pubs excepted).

ENCOURAGING MORE TO HELP

Simply put, the essence of good pest control is to have a lot of different plants and habitats in the garden. By providing many various niches, more creatures arrive and multiply. Some of the most effective encouragements are:

Feeding stations
These range from a bird table for scraps, nut feeders for small birds, snacks for the hedgehog and loads of flowering and berrying plants to feed up all the adult insect parasites and predators. It is a good idea to put these plants where you can see them and their visitors from a window, for the pleasure this gives.

Shelter
You can help by just improving the fencing and hedging, which will make the garden warmer. Evergreens give many small creatures a temporary or permanent home; thickets, scrubby bushes and even tussocks of grass are all important to some inhabitants. On the smallest scale, rough chunky bark mulches and straw encourage spiders and beetles.

Bird baths and frog ponds
Water is essential for every living thing and birds will eat less fruit and seedlings if they can easily get a drink. Many other creatures need water either to breed in or hide in, and small pools and ponds help keep many pests down by breeding up predators such as frogs, toads, newts, dragonflies and beetles.

Beetle bunds
Beetles are particularly useful; the vast majority are our friends and many eat pests and pest eggs. The most important ground-dwelling carnivorous ones are easily increased in numbers by leaving strips of grass to grow long. Make these doubly useful by filling the strips up with spring bulbs and flowers (see also chapter 3).

Aphid hosts
Aphids are continually under attack from many predators and parasites and it is rare they get out of control. They do occasionally need direct action from a hose-pipe jet of water or a soft-soap spray but generally ladybirds, lacewings and so on do a better job with no effort on our part. We can encourage even more of these predators by growing flowers to provide pollen and nectar for the adults, and also by growing plants deliberately to breed up more aphids. These sacrificial plants, such as lupins, vetches and honeysuckles, breed more aphids, which then breed up more controlling insects that go on to prevent aphid attacks on other more important plants.

Bee sanctuaries
Just a pile of old logs, or stones or even a rubbish heap can be a good sanctuary for wild solitary bees. These pollinate flowers early in the year when honey bees can't fly and save us the trouble. A muddy bank by a pool, a heap of sand and a bundle of hollow stems all suit different sorts of bees.

Winter quarters
These can be just odd piles of detritus such as recommended above for bees. They can also be bundles of prunings, especially hollow ones, hidden inside evergreens and dense hedges. This is a very useful way of using troublesome prunings. Old piles of wood, bark even a load of bricks and rubble can provide small niches for creatures to live or hibernate in. It is only sensible to put such piles well away from susceptible plants such as hostas or salad crops as, after all, slugs and snails can't walk as far as hedgehogs and beetles.

Below: Hedgehogs are great friends if a bit noisy.

OUTWITTING PESTS

Wit and cunning can also be used to make sure that we get our crops despite the pests, by using their habits against them and without us having to do much work. A plastic sheet or a carpet laid on a grass path overnight will bring up many pests. Roll it back in the early morning and leave them for the birds. Slugs and snails can be lured onto lettuce or cabbage leaves placed as sacrificial rings around new plantings and the pests can be picked off by torch light.

Red spider mites on greenhouse plants can be lured onto broad bean seedlings in pots: once the mites have taken up residence they can be removed with the bean plants and destroyed. Likewise, whitefly can be lured onto sweet tobacco plants and then sprayed with sugar solution or hair lacquer and removed. Mealy bugs can be lured onto sprouting potatoes. Wood lice congregate under hollowed out potatoes or orange skins and are easiest to catch with a hand-held vacuum cleaner. A vacuum cleaner can also be used to thin out populations of flying pests such as whitefly, but then this is getting too much like work...

Ants can be fooled into bringing up their cocoons or eggs, as we call them, into tin cans placed over their nests. The ants bring the eggs up into the warmth on a sunny day and take them down at night. So in the early afternoon we can steal them to feed to wild birds, fish or hens. Doing this several times weakens the nest so it can be finished off with boiling water.

However, I have always disliked killing things and then one day I had an idea. I was watching a nature documentary about tropical ants and some of these lived in harmony with certain plants. The plants gave the ants a sweet sap and in return the ants kept all the pests off the plant. Now I had a coldframe that for several years had harboured a colony of ants that had persistently farmed crops of aphids on the sweet peppers and other plants I grew inside. So, thinking of the tropical ants, and their example I tried putting drops of jam on the stem joints of the next crop of peppers every time I watered them. Well, of course, the ants soon found the jam. The aphids appeared but then rapidly left again and I can only assume the ants ate them. Fed up with a diet of jam the ants no longer wanted to farm aphids for their sweet honeydew but looked on them instead as a nice protein snack of high-grade meat. This is only surmise but it seemed to work and I repeated it on greenhouse perennials. So try giving the ants jam and they may keep your pests down in exchange.

TAMED WILDLIFE

Over the millennia we have actually tamed many creatures of the wild and persuaded some of them to do things for us. Horses, donkeys and camels have become beasts of burden, while others such as sheep, goats and cattle have enabled us to maintain open grassland habitats by grazing off the trees for us. We have trained sheep dogs, to go out and round up the ewes for us and bees collect nectar and turn it into honey. Fishermen around the world have made their catches with the help of otters and birds and, in many countries, monkeys collect fruits and throw down coconuts from the trees.

I dream of the squirrels picking my nuts and popping them in boxes for me – there are stories of attics collapsing as nuts have been popped into a knothole for years until the weight was too much. Mice and voles nibble the seed heads of plants and collect these and make stores of fruits and berries – so far for

Below: They don't work fast but I don't pay them much.

their purposes only and not yet for mine. And instead of eating my brassicas and pea seedlings, the pigeons and doves could be weeding out the cruciferous weeds for me.

I've even found a use for snails. Just as you can have a worm composter, I have made a snail farm where they eat wastes and turn it into fertility for me. They're confined in a plastic laundry basket, moated to stop wee ones escaping, and given old drainpipes to live in. They have a saucer of fresh water and a tray of calcified seaweed. I put lettuce and cabbage leaves and fruit peelings etc, in the top and every night they eat them. Each day their droppings are washed out the bottom and used as a liquid feed. You can even do something similar with woodlice: put them in a ventilated but escape-proof place and they will shred all manner of materials down into a fine powder, and produce thousands more woodlice. Then they go to fatten the chickens, which mine do of their own accord if they escape as their 'prison' is in the hen run.

This is my ultimate aim: to have almost all the gardening tasks done for me by some creature or other making its own living.

GETTING OTHERS TO DO THE WORK FOR YOU

There may be exceptions, but apparently only rarely do the next generation inherit the same love of gardening. Even more rarely are children ever any help, especially if there are several. I've heard it said one child can be nearly as much help as half a man but two are no help at all. Hired help is also a risky business; there are few industries where unemployed actors, crooks, cowboys and layabouts can so readily bluff their way by calling themselves 'tree surgeons', 'landscape designers' and 'expert gardeners'. Hiring someone without personal recommendation is downright foolish, and leaving them unobserved (at first) is worse.

One lady called me in to ask what she could do. She had had an herbaceous border but all the plants were now gone to the compost heap and the only living thing left in the bed was ground elder. She'd employed a lad for a day to 'tidy up' the garden.

Above: Young chickens can be as fun as any other pet but never get housetrained!

A good assistant gardener is hard to find; instead hire a straight-forward labourer to do heavy tasks such as digging or laying slabs. Use a contractor (with insurance) who hires tools with operatives for big tasks; possibly employ someone to cut the grass or even maybe the hedge, but do not trust anyone with your most precious plants until you are sure of their capabilities.

In a similar vein I'm often asked by letter or in person how a son, daughter or friend who loves gardening can best be got work in some area of horticulture. I plead with them not to do so. Growing plants is a wonderful hobby, an education, a pleasure, even a means of improving your table but a hard way to earn a living that will leave no time for the original enjoyment. No, instead help find them a humble home with a generous garden and some righteous employment that only demands four days a week and gives them three to garden in. I'm sure they will be the more contented for it. (And, really, you know three days labour, three days gardening and one of rest and thanksgiving sounds even better.)

PROCESSING SENSE

The least-work storage method is to turn plant material and wastes into chickens, geese, rabbits, goats... All of these animals were developed as food preservation methods; we feed food now to the creature and later we eat it, or its eggs or milk. The development of animal husbandry parallels farming and gardening, but was not always integrated or compatible with them. For example, the problem of grazing herds destroying people's fields and moving on caused many a war. Nonetheless feeding creatures with summer fodder does convert it into something you can eat, or move, or sell later and applies to us today.

Sadly all these four-footed fiends are not suited to a small modern garden, though bunnies in cages or movable runs may be an exception if well managed. The fowls however are much more use and less dangerous to our plants. A few hens will convert garden and household weeds, refuse and wastes into eggs, feathers, chicken meat and rich droppings with very little effort on our part. I cannot recommend hens too highly as a recycling scheme; everyone ought to have a few, they are less work than a pet dog and their eggs are much better. Ducks are similar but need a pond to be happy; they don't scratch like hens so can be given free run of a garden. Geese eat grass and need lots of it, and are ideal if you have much turf to control. They will do most of the mowing for you and love to eat weeds such as dandelions, goosegrass, buttercups and clovers, so are also useful for clearing the vegetable bed and rough land. (They like carrots, globe artichokes and brassicas too, so be warned!)

HUMANE ALTERNATIVES

Of course, you might find giving a chicken a life in order to eat it offensive, so fortunately there are other ways of storing the food from your garden. Naturally it is mostly best fresh, and to save work much can be left in situ in areas where winters are mild. Leeks, parsnips, carrots and other roots, Brussels sprouts, kales, Jerusalem artichokes and hardy saladings under cloches are usually left in the ground till required. The roots are best protected from hard frosts (and made liftable) by covering them

Opposite: Winter bird food is good value for money.
Above: Muscovy ducks do little damage in my garden but do eat a lot of slugs and snails.

with a layer of dry shredded newspaper, straw or similar, and keeping it dry and snug with a weighed down plastic sheet. Cabbages and cauliflowers can be covered individually with multiple layers of newspaper and plastic bags and left in situ. In hard winter areas these crops all need taking under cover in a shed or cellar.

I use dead deep freezers as insulated storage containers for keeping many different crops. They are ideal for cabbages, potatoes, apples and so on, as the constant humidity and temperature preserves these all well and the metal walls keep out rats and mice. Some crops such as onions and garlic can just be hung in dry frost-free places and many crops, especially fruits, are easily dried, frozen, jellied and jammed. But all that is far too much labour for most people. I'm happy to do it but few are as foolish. In terms of least labour, then drying is pretty efficient: the food needs preparing and once dry is simply packed in a jar. Freezing requires some care but is not too much effort for fruits; blanching vegetables makes it barely worth the effort. Juicing and freezing the juices is little work in total for generous results, as storage losses are low. Wine making is another possiblity.

TURN YOUR WATERING INTO WINE

One of the most ancient ways of storing fruits was to turn them into wine. The techniques are out of the scope of this book, and although relatively easy, I don't recommend wine making. (Though cider is so much easier to make a tasty brew I do recommend that.) However, you can turn your watering into wine in a more subtle way. You see, us gardeners are such generous folk, we can't resist giving away our hard-won produce to all and sundry. And bigger fools we are if we give away the best fruits and superb vegetables, which we invariably do, only to eat the second-rate ourselves. Now, as I have said before I don't wish to be uncharitable, but what is the use of giving your friends a big basket of produce if they will just leave it to wilt and wither, as I have seen done too often. Nowadays, if it doesn't have a microwave instruction printed on the side some folk don't know how to cook it. Now instead I invite friends round for meals. This way I make sure they benefit from my organic food.

Below: Another useful friend.

If you cook it, you don't need to ensure the produce looked impeccable before it was peeled, so now the best can be stored to be eaten later. Of course, what do friends do when they come for a meal? They bring a bottle of wine as the usual token of appreciation, and with much cajoling, mine have now been

> You see, us gardeners are such generous folk, we can't resist giving away our hard-won produce to all and sundry.

persuaded to bring organic wine. To be honest, I can make very good fruit juice but my wine has not often been top rate: drinkable, yes; effective, yes; but highly pleasurable, no. So I cook for my friends, the food is magnificent and the best bit is I can enjoy their fine wine with it while my friends cannot, as they're driving home and I've only got to stagger to my bed.

IT'S NOT WORK IF...

There is a difference between a task, a job, some work to do or a chore. The same occupation may be pleasant or onerous, and this can depend as much on one's attitude as on the actual activity. For example, although cutting a hedge can be hard dusty work and a hard way to make a living, it can also be quite enjoyable if done in an unrushed relaxed manner, gently with shears and refreshment. Likewise I, a confirmed bachelor, no lover of housework, once found myself whistling as I was vacuuming, dusting and cleaning windows. Why? Well, need it be said that I was anticipating entertaining a lovely lady I had met and of course my den had to be mucked out so to speak. But I'd caught myself whistling, an indication of contentment if ever there was one, yet I was doing chores I abhorred. Yes, but doing them with joy in my heart. Admittedly this was aided and abetted by male lust, but nonetheless it demonstrated to me one of the most important lessons regarding work in the garden – and everywhere else: when you set to it with good heart, it's never work but a pleasure.

Right: Squiggly, hard at work...

making it easier throughout the year

There is a very old saying, 'a stitch in time saves nine.' This is true in almost everything and particularly so in gardening. Many a pest outbreak can initially be squashed between finger and thumb, but before long the eggs have hatched and the maggots moved apart all over the plants. Indeed, much of the skill and relaxed attitude of the 'good old boys' is that they are well aware of the timing for each and every operation.

Much of the knowledge a gardener needs soon comes with a few years' experience of doing the right thing but at the wrong time! (Of course, you could also be doing the wrong thing at the right time with equally mixed results, but it doesn't matter as long as you learn from the experience and do better next time.) Basically, it is much like learning to drive. Initially it is all panic, soon things make some sense and before long you are looking further ahead and it all becomes automatic. Until then, here are some methods and reminders of what must be done when.

The round of rounds

To maintain a garden, many just do what happens to take their notice at any time but then things get missed. To avoid this error there is a simple method: keep a diary of missed opportunities. Whenever you find you have forgotten to do something, make a note of it in a spare diary to prevent this

recurring next year. Put each note in the week or month the task ought to be done. This will accumulate over the years into your own personal prompter, though with experience, it should become needed less often.

And everything in gardening is cyclical and comes round and round again. To make it easier to cope with each job in its turn, we can break down the tasks into those that need doing really frequently, those that need doing regularly, and those that are seasonal and only come round once or so a year.

The daily round Make a daily inspection tour and go round the garden writing a 'to do' list of approaching and most urgent jobs (notes such as 'sowings', 'potting-ups', or 'prunings due'), so these may be planned at leisure. As you progress, water whatever is wanting, and harvest whatever is needed, for the kitchen or storage. Also simultaneously collect and dispose of all litter, collect up other junk, tools, toys, etc, and put them away. If you have a coldframe or greenhouse then, depending on the season, open and close the ventilation and/or check the min/max. thermometer to ensure sufficiently effective heating and cooling.

The weekly routine The vital tasks are daily ones; only once these are completed should you start on the weekly chores. The most important of these is to hit any window for sowing and transplanting – next week will be too late. Afterwards, sharpen your hoe and weed the beds and borders. Once these are done, clip the lawn edges and mow the grass. Then collect all suitable materials together for composting and move them to the heap. Have a break, sit down and think, before starting on any seasonal tasks due that you have carefully noted down during the week such as fruit thinning or compost turning.

The seasonal cycle As everything in gardening is dictated by the season, then along with the regular jobs such as the watering, weeding and grass cutting, there are a variety of activities that only come round once each year, such as harvesting in autumn and the preparations for winter. These are often easier to overlook than the more frequent tasks so here I've listed the most important. Obviously, the exact timing varies with locality, site and soil, but most plants have similar requirements at much the same times. And these are done by season, with the gardener's year naturally starting off in darkest coldest late winter.

THE YEARLY DIARY OR CALENDAR OF PASS-TIMES

Late Winter

- Check straps and stakes on trees after gales.

- Empty insect traps and old bird boxes.

- Hang bird boxes before they need them.

- Put out bird food, hang up fat and provide water.

- Check your fruit and vegetable stores; remove anything starting to rot before it infects others.

- Put down impenetrable sheet mulches on top of new ground or sow green manures.

- Spread loose mulches under and around everything, preferably immediately after a period of heavy rain.

- Spray peaches and almonds with Bordeaux mixture against peach leaf curl disease when buds are swelling.

- If no frosts are forecast, cut grass with blades set high and return the clippings to the lawn to feed the worms.

- If ground is workable, plant out hardy trees and shrubs that missed autumn planting.

- Firm in roots of autumn plantings after hard frosts.

- Do major pruning work missed earlier, but not to stone fruits or evergreens unless damaged by winter storms.

- Make sure no weeds are getting away; they pull up easily at this time: hoe whenever it's dry enough.

- Tidy sheds and greenhouses, repair and clean tools and equipment.

- Order seeds and plants if you've not done so already and plan their positions.

- Chit early seed potatoes on trays in a light, frost-free place.

Early Spring

- Check your fruit and vegetable stores, remove anything starting to rot before it infects others.

- Examine each and every plant in your care for pests, diseases and dieback before they start to leaf up.

- Put out food, hang up fat and provide water for birds.

- Once ground becomes workable, plant out evergreens, soft fruit, artichokes, asparagus, and rhubarb.

- Prune tender plants, evergreens, herbs and hollow stemmed shrubs such as buddleias.

- Make sure no weeds get away, hoe every other week at least and add extra mulch on top of thin mulches with soil or small weeds starting to show.

- Cut the grass at least fortnightly, preferably weekly, returning the clippings or putting them around trees and bushes.

- Move, lay, sow and repair turf in non-frosty weather.

- Spray the whole garden with diluted seaweed solution.

- Spray peaches and almonds for the second time with Bordeaux mixture.

- Pollinate early-flowering plants under cover by hand.

- On still cold nights, protect blossoms and young fruitlets from frost damage with net curtains or sheets.

- Sow plants to be grown under cover: tomatoes, cucumbers, aubergines, peppers, hardy and half-hardy annual flowering plants.

- Plant outdoors: garlic, onion sets, shallots, potatoes.

- Sow outdoors in warm soil under cloches: peas, broad beans, onions, leeks, beetroot, kohl rabi, cabbages, cauliflowers, lettuces, spinach, turnips, carrots, chards, salsify, scorzonera, parsnips, herbs, radishes, spring onions, sweet peas and hardy annuals.

Mid spring

- Use up stored fruits and vegetables; clean out empty stores.

- Examine each and every plant in your care for early signs of pests and diseases.

- Put out slug and pheromone traps if you think it worth the expense.

- Firm in roots of earlier plantings after any hard frosts.

- Make sure no weeds are getting away; hoe weekly.

- Cut the grass weekly, returning the clippings to the lawn or putting them around trees and bushes.

- Spray everything with diluted seaweed solution and anything showing deficiency symptoms more heavily.

- De-flower new fruit plants to give them time to establish.

- Protect blossoms and young fruitlets from frost with net curtains, plastic sheets or newspaper.

- Feed and top dress all plants in pots.

- Tie in new growths of vines and climbing plants.

- Prune and cut back most early flowering shrubs once flowers have died.

- Outdoors sow: peas, broad beans, most brassicas, lettuces and saladings, herbs, spinach, turnips, carrots, swedes, salsify, scorzonera, radishes, kohl rabi, fennel, leeks, parsnips, sweet peas and hardy annuals.

- Plant out potatoes, onion seedlings, perennial herbs.

- Sow plants grown under cover for later planting out; tomatoes, ridge cucumbers, gherkins, courgettes, marrows, pumpkins, sweet corn and half hardy flowers.

- Make night-time inspections of your garden, especially the sowing and propagation area, looking for slugs, snails, wood lice, vine weevils and cutworms; arm yourself with a jar of soapy or salty water in which to drown them.

Late spring

● Examine each and every plant for pests and diseases, especially aphids, caterpillars, and, indoors, red spider mite or whitefly.

● Pot up any plant needing re-potting.

● Make sure no weeds are getting away; hoe frequently, adding extra mulch on top of mulches with weeds growing in them.

● Cut the grass at least fortnightly, preferably weekly, returning the clippings or putting them around potatoes.

● Establish a watering round for all pot-grown plants, at least daily. Feed indoor pot plants with comfrey liquid or seaweed solution weekly.

● Spray everything with diluted seaweed solution, and anything with deficiency symptoms more heavily.

● On still cold nights, protect blossoms and young fruitlets from frost damage.

● Cut back most flowering shrubs once flowers die.

● Tie in and support climbers and tallest herbaceous plants.

● Harden off and plant out in greenhouse or polytunnel: tomatoes, peppers, aubergines, melons, sweet corn, ridge cucumbers, courgettes and marrows. Or plant them outside under cloches if sure last frost is over.

● Sow in situ under cloches outdoors once sure frosts are over: tomatoes, ridge cucumbers, gherkins, courgettes, marrows, pumpkins, French beans, runner beans, sweet corn and half-hardy flowers.

● Outdoors without cloches sow: peas, most brassicas, lettuces and saladings, herbs, spinach, turnips, carrots, swedes, salsify, scorzonera, kohl rabi, fennel, leeks, parsnips and hardy annual and biennial flowers.

● Harvest and use, or store and preserve, any crops.

● Make night-time inspections of your garden for pests.

Early summer

- Examine each and every plant for pests and diseases, especially aphids, caterpillars and, indoors, red spider mite or whitefly.

- Pot up anything needing re-potting.

- Ensure good weed control; make sure no weeds are getting away; hoe fortnightly or weekly.

- Increase frequency of watering for all pot-grown plants to at least three times daily.

- Feed indoor pot plants with comfrey liquid or seaweed solution weekly.

- Plant out or move out for summer, tender plants in pots. Cut the grass at least fortnightly, preferably weekly, but raise the height of cut of the mower.

- Spray everything growing with diluted seaweed solution, and anything with deficiency symptoms more heavily.

- Deadhead roses and cut back most flowering plants after flowers die.

- Thin raspberry canes.

- Prune grapevines back to three or five leaves after a flower truss.

- Tie in new growths of climbing plants.

- Fruit thinning: do the first selection by removing every diseased, decayed, damaged, misshapen, distorted and congested fruitlet. Compost or burn rejected fruitlets immediately, then protect rest from birds.

- Sow outdoors: lettuces and saladings, beetroot, kohl rabi, swedes, turnips, spinach, chicory, endive and biennial and perennial flowers.

- Harvest and use, or store and preserve, everything before it disappears.

Mid summer

- Make sure no weeds are getting away; hoe fortnightly.

- Water all pot-grown plants at least three times daily
Feed pot plants with comfrey liquid or seaweed solution weekly.

- Cut the grass at least fortnightly, preferably weekly, but raise the height of cut of mower even more.

- Spray everything growing with diluted seaweed solution, and anything with deficiency symptoms more heavily.

- Deadhead roses and cut back most flowering plants after flowers die.

- Spray maincrop potatoes with Bordeaux mixture against blight if warm and humid.

- Summer pruning: remove approximately half to three quarters of each new shoot, except for leaders, of all red and whitecurrants, gooseberries and all trained fruit. Prune grapevines back to three or five leaves after a flower truss, if no flower truss by sixth leaf stop anyway and mark for later removal. Blackcurrants need old wood removing once fruited, raspberries likewise. Stone fruits are traditionally pruned now to avoid silver leaf disease.

- Tie in new growths of climbing plants.

- Cut back evergreens and conifer hedges.

- Fruit thinning, second go: remove damaged fruits. Harvest and use, or preserve ripe fruits and protect every remaining fruit from birds and wasps.

- Sow outdoors: lettuces and saladings, carrots, swedes, turnips, Chinese cabbage, winter spinach, kohl rabi, Florence fennel, chards.

- Harvest and use or store everything.

- Make night-time inspections of your garden for pests.

Late summer

- Reduce water for pot grown plants to at least twice daily. Feed pot plants with comfrey liquid or seaweed solution weekly.

- Cut the grass at least fortnightly, preferably weekly, but reduce the height of cut of the mower a little.

- Spray everything growing with diluted seaweed solution, and anything with deficiency symptoms more heavily.

- Deadhead roses and cut back most flowering plants after flowers die.

- Stone fruits should have been pruned by now to avoid Silver leaf disease.

- Tie in new growths of climbing plants.

- Plant new strawberry plants, if you can get them.

- Protect every ripening fruit from birds and wasps.

- Order hardy trees and shrubs for autumn planting.

- Sow under cover: winter lettuces and saladings, early carrots, outdoors winter lettuces and saladings, Japanese and spring onions, winter spinach, turnips, Chinese greens and hardy and biennial flowers

- Sow green manures and winter ground cover on bare soil that is not mulched.

- Harvest and use, store or preserve everything.

Early autumn

- Decrease watering for all pot-grown plants, but still check daily.

- Ensure good weed control, make sure no weeds are getting away; hoe fortnightly or add extra mulch on top.

- Transplant pot-grown biennial-flowering plants and those with a decent rootball.

- Plant outside: garlic, daffodils and most other bulbs.

- Sow hardy annuals to overwinter.

- Sow green manures and grass.

- Cut the grass at least fortnightly, preferably weekly, collecting the clippings with any fallen leaves and putting them around trees and bushes. Raise the height of cut again.

- Cut back herbaceous plants as their stems wither.

- Remove old canes and tie in new on all berries.

- On still cold nights, protect tender bedding plants from frost damage with sheets.

- Bring tender plants in pots indoors.

- Collect and dry seeds.

- Harvest and use or store everything before it goes.

Mid Autumn

● Decrease watering further as growth slows more.

● Make sure no weeds are getting away; hoe fortnightly or add extra mulch on top.

● Plant outside garlic and bulbs, deciduous shrubs, trees and soft fruit, preferably bare rooted

● Cut the grass at least fortnightly, preferably weekly, collecting clippings and fallen leaves together or raking them into rings around trees and bushes.

● Aerate and spike the grass if needed, adding sharp sand and grass seed if a true workaholic.

● Check straps and stakes on trees before any gales.

● Cut back herbaceous plants as their stems wither.

● Winter prune apples, pears, grapes and non-stone fruits and other plants once they drop their leaves.

● Make new beds and borders and move turf.

● Spread mulches under and around everything possible.

● Order seed catalogues and anything to plant soon.

● Check stores and remove anything starting to rot before it infects others.

● Harvest and store late fruits and tender root vegetables .

● Collect and dry seeds and berries for sowing next year and to feed birds.

Late autumn

● Water only as needed for all pot-grown plants.

● Still make sure no weeds are getting away; hoe fortnightly or add extra mulch on top.

● Cut the grass at least fortnightly collecting the fallen leaves with the clippings or raking them onto now empty or dormant beds and borders.

● Lime the vegetable beds.

● Make and turn compost heaps; sieve and store compost too.

● Plant out bare-rooted deciduous shrubs, trees and soft fruit if soil is in good condition and they are dormant.

● Winter prune anything still needing it.

● Check straps and stakes on trees after any gales.

● Take cuttings of hardy plants as they drop their leaves.

● Harvest and store root vegetables under cover in cold areas.

● Check stores and remove anything starting to rot before it infects others.

● Take all hosepipes and plastic cans, etc, under cover before hard frosts make them brittle.

Early winter

● Decrease watering of pot-grown plants to minimum as growth almost stops.

● Plant out hardy trees and bushes if soil still in good condition and not frozen.

● Check straps and stakes on trees after each gale.

● Cut the grass if weather still mild; collect the fallen leaves with the few clippings and bag them for leaf mould.

● Lime most tough grass swards every fourth year except among ericaceous plants or lime haters.

● Clean out gutters and drains once last leaves have fallen.

● Clean greenhouse, coldframe and cloche glass and plastic.

● Prune hardy trees and bushes and do major work to trees and bushes (but not to stone fruits or evergreens).

● Make a bonfire of diseased and thorny material.

● Check stores and remove anything starting to rot before it infects others.

● Get your seed orders in early so you get the best choice and they arrive in time for the new season.

● Order seeds, potatoes, evergreen and herbaceous plants for spring.

Mid winter

● On clear bright days make a health and hygiene check and examine each and every plant in your care for damage and dieback, scale insects and mummified fruits.

● Check straps and stakes on trees after any gales.

● Check stores and remove anything starting to rot.

● Collect up and destroy hibernating snails.

● Make bird boxes, slug pubs, insect traps, hibernation quarters and plastic bottle cloches.

● Clean and repair the mower so it's ready to roll.

● Make sure your seed orders are in.

● Relax, take it easy for a while; note your successes and mishaps, enjoy the fruits of your labours, and plan as much pleasure next year doing even less work.

APPENDIX

Other publications by the same author:

Bob Flowerdew's Organic Bible
A comprehensive tour de force. This manual contains all you could ever want to know about organic gardening and the wonderful results of working with nature, the flowers and the produce and tending the harmonious space they live in with us.

All the photographs in this book were taken in Bob Flowerdew's garden by Christine Mackenzie Topping; a garden photographer well known for her plant portraits featured in Express Newspapers, *Radio Times*, *Amateur Gardening* and *Kitchen Garden* magazines.

Bob Flowerdew's Complete Fruit Book
for the US re-titled *The Complete Book Of Fruit*
in Holland as *Alles over Fruit*
in France as *Le Livre des fruits*
in Czech as *Ovoce velka kniha plodu*
also in German and Polish.

This book has all you could ever wish to know about growing and eating every fruit and nut, from the common and the garden to the wild and exotic. Published by Kyle Cathie.

The Companion Garden sadly now out of print.
for the US re-titled *The Good Companions*

A concise introduction to the way plants may be used to help each other. Published by Kyle Cathie.

Bob Flowerdew's Complete Book of Companion Gardening.
Revised edition. (7th) available in paperback

Published by Kyle Cathie.

The Organic Gardener now out of print.

also known as *Bob Flowerdew's Organic Garden* also out of print published by Hamlyn Octopus and in France as *Le Jardin Ecologique*, published by La Maison Rustique, and in Spain as *El Jardín Orgánico* published by Gustavo Gili. Re-issued in a new and revised form for 2002 as *Go Organic* also by Hamlyn Octopus.

also Bob co-authored
The Complete Manual of Organic Gardening published by Headline
and
Gardeners' Question Time published by Orion

INDEX

PHOTOGRAPHIC ACKNOWLEDGEMENTS

The publisher would like to thank the following for permission to use photographs in the book.

Mark Bolton: 8, 31

Jonathon Buckley: 33, 79, 85 (right), 96, 181

Garden Exposures: 26–7, 58 (top left), 89 (left)

Garden Matters: 11, 30, 43, 53 (top), 60 (top), 66, 83, 97, 101

Garden Picture Library: 2–3 (Martin Mauchy), 12 (Jacqui Hurst), 28 (Janet Sorrell), 37 (Mayer/Le Scanff), 62 (J. Sira), 63 (Juliette Wade), 64 (Steven Wooster), 67 (Sunniva Harte), 68 (Mayer/Le Scanff), 114, 116 (Clive Nichols/Chelsea 1999), 128 (top) (Harold Rice), 131 (Mel Watson), 132 (bottom)(Andrea Jones), 133 (Neil Holmes), 135 (Mayer/Le Scanff), 138 (John Glover), 140 (Photo Lamontagne), 149 (Bridget Thomas), 151 (Joanna Pavia), 153 (Michael Howes), 157 (Jacqui Hurst), 159 (Juliette Wade), 169 (Ron Sutherland), 172 (Clive Nichols), 174 (Ron Sutherland)

John Glover: 15 (design: Steve Woodham), 22, 24 (design: Steve Woodham), 35, 65, 70, 112, 118, 123, 126, 127 (top right and bottom),129, 132 (bottom), 137, 142 (garden: Lotusland, Santa Barbara, California), 144, 168, 186

Jerry Harpur: 1, 23, 29, 41, 56, 59 (Stonecrop), 73, 80 (Stellenberg, Cape Town), 98, 111, 119, 143, 165, 179 (owner: Andrew Weaving, London)

Marcus Harpur: 177

Sunniva Harte: 44

Jacqui Hurst: 17 (Herterton House Nursery).

Photo Lamontagne: 32, 38, 40, 42 (bottom), 46, 53 (bottom), 59 (bottom), 85 (top), 88, 93, 94, 102, 104, 105, 154.

Andrew Lawson: 42 (top), 58 (bottom) (designer: Land Art), 61, 75, 78, 81, 84 (Bingerden, Holland), 86, 146.

Christine Mackenzie Topping: 117, 120, 121, 124, 127, 130, 145, 148, 156, 163, 166, 170, 171, 173, 175, 178 and back cover author photograph.

Marianne Majerus: 34, 58, 182.

S and O Mathews: 6–7, 9, 50, 76, 82, 90, 103, 106, 108, 180.

Mayer/Le Scanff: 51, 52, 99, 122

Clay Perry: 113, 128

Derek St. Romaine: 48 (Cleve West), 87 (RHS Rosemoor), 89 right (Mr Wainwright), 140, 147(RHS Hampton Court/Leyhill Prison), 176 (Maureen Thompson)